WONDERS OF MAN

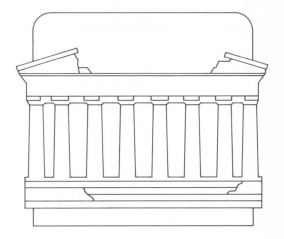

THE PARTHENON

by Peter Green

and the Editors
of the Newsweek Book Division

NEWSWEEK, New York

NEWSWEEK BOOK DIVISION

JOSEPH L. GARDNER   *Editor*

Janet Czarnetzki   *Art Director*

Edwin D. Bayrd, Jr.   *Associate Editor*
Laurie P. Phillips   *Picture Editor*
Kathleen Berger   *Copy Editor*
Susan Storer   *Picture Researcher*
Russell Ash   *European Correspondent*

S. ARTHUR DEMBNER   *Publisher*

WONDERS OF MAN

MILTON GENDEL   *Consulting Editor*

Mary Ann Joulwan   *Designer, The Parthenon*

Endpapers:
*Slanting afternoon sunlight
accentuates the geometrical
simplicity of the Parthenon's
outermost colonnade*

Title page:
*Honey-colored and weatherworn, the
Parthenon crowns Athens's ancient
citadel, the rubble-strewn, sere, and
treeless Acropolis.*

Opposite:
*A fragile wreath of beaten gold,
created in the fourth century B.C.,
about a century after the Parthenon
itself was completed*

ISBN: Clothbound Edition 0–88225–026–4
ISBN: Deluxe Edition 0–88225–027–2
Library of Congress Catalog Card No. 72–75998
© 1973 — Arnoldo Mondadori Editore, S.p.A.
All rights reserved. Printed and bound in Italy.

Contents

Introduction

As the symbolic birthplace of Western democracy, the Athenian Acropolis is the most hallowed — and the most universally acclaimed — temple site in all of Europe. The dimensions of this outcropping are unimposing, but its precipitous slopes are capped by the fragmentary remains of a half dozen major structures, among them the fabled Parthenon — a building whose familiar form has become virtually synonymous with the boldest triumphs and highest ambitions of the Age of Pericles. Indeed, the author of the engrossing narrative that follows calls the Parthenon "a precipitate and distillation of Western culture," one that summarizes the dazzling creative impact of Greece's Golden Age.

Built in the fifth century B.C. to commemorate Athens's hard-won victory over Persia, the Parthenon actually served its original purpose for less than fifty years. During that time it functioned as both a brightly painted temple to the city's guardian deity, Athena, and an exuberant expression of civic pride. It boasted pedimental sculptures (detail at left) of consummate beauty and a central cult statue of ivory and gold, all created under the supervision of Phidias, the paramount sculptor of ancient Attica.

Denuded and defiled by a succession of conquerors — Roman, Byzantine, Frankish, Catalan, Florentine, and Ottoman — and later picked clean by equally rapacious archaeologists and souvenir hunters, the once-splendid temple has gradually been reduced to a whited shell. What endures is little more than a skeleton, and sadly incomplete at that. But even so reduced, the Parthenon casts an imposing shadow, one that suggests not only Phidias's design and Pericles's dream but also the grace and vigor of Greece at its apogee.

THE EDITORS

11

Athena the warrior-maiden, triumphant symbol of Periclean Athens, cast in bronze in the fourth century B.C.

THE PARTHENON IN HISTORY

I

ATHENS ASCENDANT

Long before they reach the city outskirts, visitors to Athens see the Parthenon — that familiar, columned symbol crowning its rock, honey golden in the crystalline light of Attica, and gap-toothed where, in September 1687, a Turkish powder magazine exploded and blew the heart of it into scattered marble shards. The Parthenon is everywhere: it beckons, against a cobalt sky, down most of Athens's long and crowded boulevards. A precipitate and distillation of Western culture, it encapsulates the whole dazzling creative impact that Periclean Athens still projects across the centuries. Today, as then, it remains a focal point of myth, inseparable from the rock on which it stands. That rock, the Acropolis, forms an archaeological and historical layer cake, not all of whose strata are tangible — a repository for the beliefs, aspirations, municipal pride, and superstitious fears of three millennia. Once in Athens, you cannot escape the Acropolis. It is, after all, why you have come — why, perhaps, Western Europe exists in its present form.

Although physically inescapable, the Acropolis lacks those features that normally make for domination. It is one of the least assertive outcrops in Attica, a mass of rough, semicrystalline limestone and red schist not much over a thousand feet long and only about half that in height — a crude, sprawling ellipse between the mountains and the sea, dwarfed on the east by the violet-crowned peaks of Hymettus and on the west by Mount Aegaleus (see map, page 63). As a panoramic vantage it cannot compete with nearby Lycabettus, a high, rocky belvedere that was supposedly dropped by the goddess Athena while she was in the process of fortifying her favorite city.

Ancient sources maintain a near-total silence concerning Lycabettus, which may have formed one of Athens's ancient boundaries but which lacked that perennial involvement in human affairs that accumulates atmosphere and tradition. The contrast with the Acropolis is striking, for there we can trace continuous occupation from Neolithic times onward: Mycenaean, Greek, Byzantine, Frankish, Catalan, Florentine, Ottoman — an organic sequence that only came to an end after 1833, when Hellenophile archaeologists stripped off two thousand years of building, topsoil, and human endeavor. Scraping back to the long-forgotten Periclean dream, they turned the Acropolis into the static museum-without-walls that it is today.

This book is a survey of the history of the Acropolis — which is also the history of Athens and, to a surprising extent, of Greece — from the earliest times to the present day. Inevitably, the climax of such a narrative comes in the fifth century B.C. and focuses upon the great temple dedicated to Athena that formed Pericles's most tangible and lasting achievement as de facto head of the Athenian state. To understand all that the Parthenon stood for means looking — literally as well as figuratively — into the pit from which it was dug. We must go back in search of more primitive shrines, back to archaic myths culled from the Bronze Age, ritual practices that filled fifth-century rationalists with embarrassment. We must trace the evolution of the Acropolis from Mycenaean fortress to proud capital of an empire. And we must trace the evolution of its guardian deities from local snake and owl totems to the great gold and ivory statue of Athena, thirty-nine feet high, that the renowned sculptor Phidias created and installed

in the Parthenon. Finally, we must follow the strange vicissitudes that rock and temple underwent during the long centuries after Athens became an academic backwater. Living on its past glories and its growing tourist trade, it was in turn sacked by Sulla, revamped and refurbished with lavish endowments by patrons like Hadrian, and rebuked by Justinian, who shut down its philosophical schools and turned the Parthenon into a Christian church.

Dedicated successively to the Holy Wisdom (Hagia Sophia) and to the Holy Mother of God, the Parthenon became, in turn, an Orthodox cathedral, a Latin cathedral, a mosque, and a powder magazine. The Propylaea, the splendid entrance to the Acropolis, did duty as a Florentine *palazzo*, while the Erechtheum was turned into a harem — a fate that befell the Parthenon itself comparatively early in its history, when Demetrius the Besieger billeted himself and his favorite courtesans there in 305 B.C.

The Acropolis has survived many sieges and suffered many alien garrisons, from hobnailed Spartans to jack-booted Nazis. The cross, the crescent, and the swastika have all flown above its ramparts. Today, with Greece once more an autonomous state, the Parthenon has achieved an unlooked-for apotheosis — not only in the imaginations of scholars, but also in the eyes of the tourists for whom the ancient structure is brilliantly floodlit each night. Bare, ravaged, naked — to a degree unconceived of by its architects — the Parthenon still strikes even a casual visitor with its cumulative historical impact, the charismatic legacy of three millennia.

The first inhabitants of Attica — called Pelasgians by Greeks of a later age — reached the region by the old

The Athenian Acropolis has been occupied without
interruption since Neolithic times, and as a result
it supports the compacted detritus of half a dozen
successive civilizations. Those stonework strata,
some laid centuries apart, are still visible in less
trafficked areas (below), and they underlie all of the
major structures that now dominate the Acropolis.
These buildings all date from the fifth century B.C.,
when Athens stood at its imperial apogee and
"Attic owls," the silver coins featuring Athena's
feathered totem (right), were the most coveted
currency in the entire Aegean.

east-coast land route from Thessaly and central Greece, the route followed by every invader in Greece's long history, Xerxes included. Excavation has revealed signs of occupation on and around the Acropolis from as early as 5000 B.C. According to the noted American archaeologist Carl Blegen, these remains "indicate an agricultural population living in fixed abodes in settled communities, possessing domesticated animals and using implements of stone and bone." The Pelasgians made competent pots and had a marked taste for steatopygous female figurines, presumably created in the interests of promoting fertility. They had been residents of the Balkan peninsula long enough to appreciate and exploit Greece's idiosyncratic features — a heavily indented coastline abounding in fjords, peninsulas, and offshore islands; natural rocky outcrops, which offered ready-made places of refuge; and abundant limestone, clay, and marble for building. In such mountainous country, pasture was short and communications hazardous, but the crisscrossing ranges formed cantons that offered protection through isolation. The sea was never far away, and somewhere in every limestone massif there lurked a natural spring.

In the coastal plain of Attica the Pelasgians found all they needed. The soil was thin, but adequate; Attica had not yet become, through deforestation and soil erosion, the "fleshless skeleton" that Plato described in the fourth century B.C. There were two small rivers, the Ilissus and the Eridanus, lush with overarching trees and leafy vegetation. Immediately beside them, sheer and uncompromising, rose the rock that was to form Athens's stronghold, holy place, and the symbol of its greatness for centuries to come. We can

picture these newcomers exploring it — nervously at first, because gods and other ghostly powers dwelt in high places and had to be propitiated if disturbed. These first settlers found slow, ominous, earth-colored snakes there, and at night the trees and bushes rang with the sounds of innumerable small hoot owls, the rock's tutelary spirits. Throughout the city's history, in myth and ritual, these mildly uncanny creatures were to remain under Athena's guardianship, and Athens's internationally honored silver coins were commonly known, because of the emblem they bore, as "Attic owls." The olive, we may safely guess, grew wild on Athena's rock from the very dawn of history.

The focus of sanctity seems always to have lain on the north side of the Acropolis. Here we find the oldest, most venerable shrines — to earthborn Erechtheus, to half-human, half-snake Cecrops, to Boutes the Ploughman — and the best evidence of Neolithic occupation. Here, in a shallow grotto, was the Clepsydra Spring; here, too, were the four caves in the rock face that have been long associated with primitive vegetation and fertility worship — even though they were consecrated to such reputable, or near-reputable, Olympian deities as Zeus, Apollo, Pan, Eros, and Aphrodite. Here, layer by slow layer, the Acropolis began to accumulate its strata of permanent occupation.

With the Early Helladic period (c. 3000–c. 1900 B.C.) came a further influx of settlers, probably from Anatolia. This group included skilled smiths who established a bronze-working center on the east coast of Attica, close to modern Raphina, and whose remains have been found on and around the Acropolis. Both the north and south slopes of the Acropolis have yielded

traces of this civilization; so has the Agora, Athens's market square and place of public assembly. At an early date, occupation of the area seems to have expanded outward from the Acropolis itself, mainly northwest toward the Eridanus. One Early Helladic house has been found nearly a mile away on the site of the Academy, the place where Plato later would expound his philosophy.

The Academy itself, which was of immemorial antiquity, contained a dozen sacred olive trees supposedly taken as slips from Athena's olive on the Acropolis. According to legend, the well-watered precinct had originally been the private estate of a hero named Akademos. It is very tempting to label the house found on this site as the country home of Akademos himself, and some archaeologists have indeed done so. In any case such discoveries, combined with excavations elsewhere, make it plain that this Early Helladic culture was not only advanced but of considerable sophistication, and its eclipse between 2100 and 1900 B.C. must be labeled a great loss. Indeed, it marked a level of civilization and achievement that was not to be reached again for another half millennium.

What happened to Greece at the close of the Early Helladic period, on the mainland and elsewhere, was once regarded as comparatively straightforward. The region found itself invaded by several waves of Indo-European migrants from beyond the Danube, men who spoke a language that was a precursor of Greek and imposed both their rule and their tongue on the pre-Hellenic population. These newcomers introduced the chariot, the fast potter's wheel, the long sword, the megaron style of building, patriarchal ethics, new burial customs, and such highly characteristic pottery as the bluish Minyan ware, distinguished by its oddly soapy texture. It is a neat, schematic pattern — but today little save the pottery and the burial customs remains unchallenged by modern scholars. Nevertheless, the basic pattern of invasion, cultural relapse, and slow assimilation can be taken as proven fact — and so can the appearance of pastoral-patriarchal mores. It was from this polarized amalgam of northern and Aegean features that the Greeks, as we know them, emerged.

For centuries Athens, like the rest of the mainland, seems to have marked time, culturally backward and economically depressed. The men who invaded Attica during the Early Helladic period knew nothing about boats or the sea, which in Greece must have proved a severe initial handicap. We know that they occupied the Acropolis and its environs, for they left characteristic traces of themselves behind. And here, as elsewhere, they developed a distinctive pattern of existence centered on the rock, or *acropolis,* and spilling out into a peripheral cluster of dwelling places. Farms and kitchen gardens lay beyond, and pasturage could be found on the slopes of the surrounding hills. Thus Athens from the beginning formed a typical Greek *polis,* or city-state, embodying elements of mountain, pasture, plain, rock, and sea. From the earliest times its king or chieftain, who was warrior, priest, judge, and ruler all in one, dwelt on the rock-fortress in a megaron-type house — that is, in an oblong double room with a pitched gable roof and a fixed hearth in the main hall. In time, this megaron style was adopted to provide homes for the rock's deities, both those of the newcomers and those already in residence. We now have

Griffins, winged leonine beasts common to early Greek mythology, decorate the ivory jewel box at right, which was carved in the fourteenth century B.C. during the ascendancy of Mycenae, the first commercially vigorous Greek city-state. The "pediment of the olive tree" (left), a fragment from an unidentified archaic structure on the Acropolis, is thought to represent the citadel's original temple to Athena, long since demolished. In any case, it suggests the design of the Mycenaean buildings that graced the Acropolis a millennium before the Parthenon itself was constructed.

present all the constituent elements, in embryonic form, of a classical acropolis — with one fundamental distinction. In later, less autocratic times no ruler lived on the rock unless he was a despot or tyrant. The absolute power conferred by this preeminent location belonged to the gods alone.

From about 1600 B.C. onward a striking change can be observed in the culture of mainland Greece, which for the next three centuries grew steadily in wealth and power. Its sudden efflorescence is symbolized by the shaft graves at Mycenae with their prodigal treasures of wrought gold and other rare objets d'art. This Late Helladic culture, which is commonly known as Mycenaean although Mycenae was never the capital of a centralized empire, first rivaled and then eclipsed the great maritime empire of Minoan Crete, which had dominated the Aegean since about 1750. Crete's main city, Cnossos, with its mighty palace, its bull cult, and its mysterious Labyrinth, finally fell around 1400. For another century Mycenaean traders sailed unchecked through the length and breadth of the Mediterranean, while Mycenaean centers on mainland Greece — Argos, Tiryns, Pylos, Athens, Thebes, and Mycenae itself — enjoyed increasing prosperity. Unlike the Minoans, the mainland barons were great warrior-hunters, and Greek mythology is largely concerned with garbled memories of their exploits.

Athens never rivaled "golden Mycenae" as a fighting barony, and the undistinguished part played by the Athenian contingent in Homer's *Iliad* subsequently caused much embarrassment to the city's more patriotic citizens. But Athens undoubtedly shared in the general prosperity, and towers, terrace walls, and postern gates

from this period have been found on the Acropolis. A palace complex was built there, close to what afterward became the Erechtheum and embracing not only the royal domestic and administrative quarters but also the sites of various early shrines and altars. A natural entrance gate was established above the more gently sloping western escarpment of the rock. Rich tombs were built and provided with offerings of gold and ivory. Imported pottery, a sure sign of affluence, became increasingly prevalent — vases from Cnossos, wine jars that originated on the Phoenician coast, and Egyptian faiences and scarabs.

That link with Egypt is of particular interest when we turn to the legendary — or, at best, quasi-historical — tradition concerning Athens's early kings. According to legend the first king of Athens was Cecrops. The date of his accession is given as 1581 B.C., and some sources claim that both he and his successor, Erechtheus, were of Egyptian origin. In this they resemble another early Greek dynast, Danaus, who is said to have left Egypt and established a kingdom in the Peloponnese about the same time. There is a very real possibility that both legends may be based on an indisputable historical fact: the expulsion of the Hyksos, or Shepherd Kings, and the mercenaries who supported them from Egypt around 1570. This hypothesis would also account for the sudden influx of wealth, in the form of plunder, to Mycenae.

These early kings of Athens — Cecrops, Erechtheus, and the rest — are, as one scholar pithily observed, "a dire confusion of duplicates, with more than a suspicion of faded gods." It was during Cecrops's reign, for example, that Athena and Poseidon supposedly had their

The legendary feats of King Agamemnon, who led the men of Mycenae to the gates of Troy in the thirteenth century B.C., completely eclipsed the achievements of his predecessors. As a result, the gold funerary mask seen below is commonly called the Agamemnon mask despite the fact that it was fashioned several centuries before his time. In actuality, Priam's conqueror is but one of a number of Mycenaean princes who were interred beneath their city's citadel. Those royal graves—the first of which was opened by Heinrich Schliemann, the rediscoverer of Troy, in 1876— have yielded a golden trove of staggering proportions and undeniable elegance. Among the hundreds of items unearthed in the vicinity of Agamemnon's fortress are the earrings at right and the graceful chalice opposite, which is banded with bounding hares.

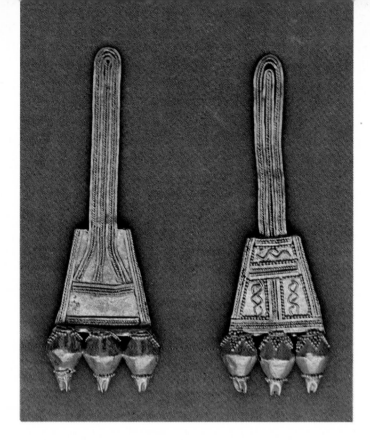

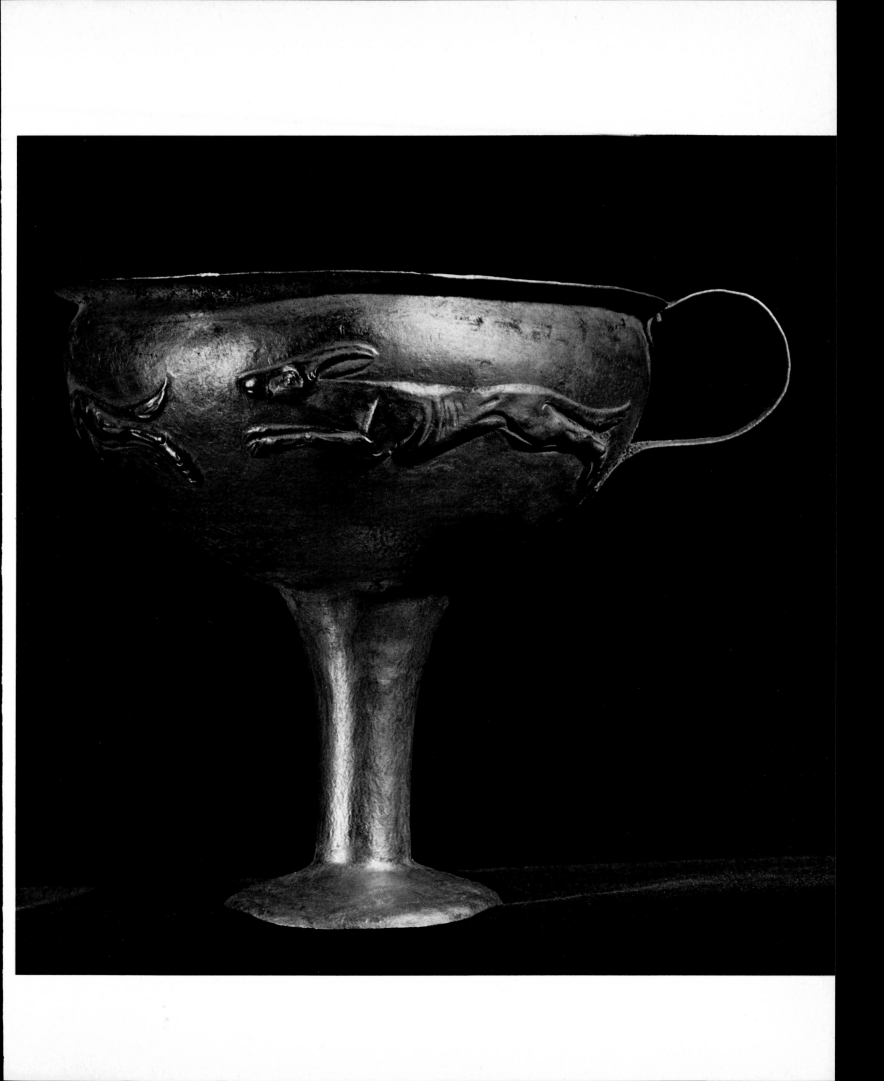

The great citadel of Tiryns lies in ruins today, its massive walls pitted by the elements and its vaulting exposed to the Peloponnesian sun (below). Formidable even in rubble, the cyclopean enceinte has been labeled the finest extant example of Mycenaean military architecture. No less formidable were the soldiers who manned that citadel, warriors who gradually extended their city-state's influence across the Aegean—often at Crete's expense and frequently at the point of a sword. Elegance and utility combine in the Mycenaean dagger blades at right, both of which are inlaid with precious metals. The upper blade is inset with a spiral pattern; the lower features a series of scenes from a lion hunt.

famous "contest for the land" to determine which of them should preside over Attica. Poseidon, god of the sea, of earthquakes, of bulls and horses, first marked the Acropolis with his trident, then produced a miraculous saltwater spring. Athena, perceiving that utilitarian gifts would prove more acceptable than mere demonstrations of supernatural power, gave Attica the olive tree — and was adjudged the winner. In any event, Cecrops, like Erechtheus, subsequently found his own niche on Athena's rock, and his tomb, the Cecropeum, could still be seen there in historical times. Athenians credit him with various civilizing statutes, among them the institution of marriage and the abolition of all forms of blood sacrifice.

Erechtheus, or Erichthonius as he was also called, was described as "earthborn," a term generally taken to mean native but perhaps no more than a reminder of his genesis as a harvest deity. According to one myth, the fire god Hephaestus sexually assaulted Athena — but failed in his purpose through premature ejaculation. The seed was quickened and gestated by Ge, the earth goddess, who bore Erichthonius on Athena's behalf. Athena entrusted the baby, whom she had enclosed in a chest, to Cecrops's three daughters, Aglauros, Pandrosos, and Herse. These Dew Maidens were given strict instructions that they should keep the chest closed, but Aglauros opened it. The sight of the infant — half child, half snake — so scared her that she jumped off the Acropolis. When he came to manhood, Erichthonius naturally took special pains to propitiate Athena: he built her a temple and he instituted a festival in her honor that afterwards became famous as the Panathenaea. Homer variously describes Athena as his

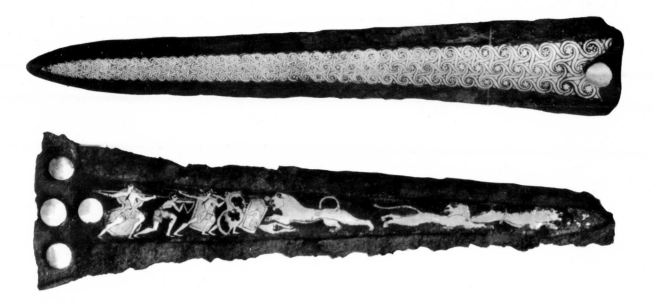

hostess in her temple and as a guest herself in Erechtheus's palace. Coexistence had clearly been established from a very early period.

Although she brought Attica the olive, Athena had no jurisdiction over grain, which more properly came under the aegis of Demeter, the patron deity of Athens's neighbor and early rival, Eleusis. It was not until 600 B.C. that Eleusis was finally absorbed into Attica, and early legend reveals sharp rivalry between the two regions. Meanwhile Athena's beneficent rule had drawn together a number of local fertility cults, among them those associated with Erechtheus-Erichthonius, Boutes the Ploughman, the Dew Maidens, and their near-doubles, the mysterious Arrhephoroi. These last appeared in historical times as young maidens who lived by the temple of Athena Polias, began the weaving of the robe for the goddess's ancient image, and may have been represented as caryatids supporting the Erechtheum porch. Moreover, the Arrhephoroi performed a curious annual ceremony, one described by the Greek travel writer Pausanias in the second century A.D.: "Having placed on their heads what the priestess of Athena gives them to carry — neither she who gives nor they who carry have any knowledge what it is — the maidens descend by the natural underground passage that goes across to the adjacent precinct within the city of Aphrodite in the Gardens. They leave down below what they carry and receive something else which they bring back covered up."

There are parallels here not only with the chest of Erichthonius but also with the Mysteries celebrated at Eleusis. In addition, both the staircase by which the girls descended and the precincts of Aphrodite have

been identified. It seems clear that the Dew Maidens received worship from a very early time, perhaps as the original Arrhephoroi. A shrine to Pandrosos survived on the Acropolis throughout the classical period, and young Athenian men, upon receiving their first arms, took the oath of allegiance in the precinct of Aglauros.

From about 1425 B.C., the beginning of that archaeological period known as Late Helladic III, our hard evidence about Athens becomes a little more plentiful, although it remains sketchy in comparison with the abundant material yielded by such major Peloponnesian sites as Mycenae and Pylos. The name that now emerges is that of the legendary Troezenian hero Theseus, sired by King Aegeus of Athens — or possibly by Poseidon himself. This ubiquitous yet curiously tangential figure turns up in countless myths, and his sexual exploits seem to have been as numerous and varied as those of his mythical rival, Heracles. Two traditions in particular linked him with Athenian history. First, he was held to have brought about the unification of Attica's twelve independent cantons under Athenian leadership. Second, he was credited with delivering Athens from some kind of obligation to Minoan Crete. It should be noted in passing that Theseus's kingship seems to have been highly insecure, and that tradition says he died in exile on Scyros. His claim to the throne was resisted by the "sons of Pallas," who regarded him as a foreign interloper.

The rich tombs scattered about Attica's country districts and datable to this period suggest that unification was, from the Athenian point of view at least, an object well worth achieving. How far Theseus can be held responsible for this project, which was not fully accom-

plished until the middle of the sixth century, is very much open to doubt. His supposedly democratic ideas are even more suspect. On the other hand, his purported dealings with Crete may well be based upon a core of half-remembered fact. Though the Minoans never ruled Athens, it was not for lack of trying: their troops invaded Attica at a time of blight and drought, and Theseus's fabled exploit against the Bull of Marathon may represent a successful drive to clear the enemy from this area. Every nine years, according to legend, seven maids and seven young men had to be sent to Minos as tribute. Theseus volunteered to join one such tribute party, seduced Minos's daughter Ariadne soon after his arrival, killed the Minotaur, and returned home in triumph, leaving Ariadne on the island of Naxos en route. Theseus's failure to switch his black sail for a triumphant white one led his aged father, Aegeus, to conclude that the expedition was a failure and to commit suicide by jumping from the Acropolis at the ship's approach.

Although most of these details sound fictitious, Theseus may well have played some part in the historical events that led to the fall of Cnossos and the eclipse of the Cretan sea empire around 1400 B.C. For a century or so thereafter, the archaeological records show peace and prosperity throughout Mycenaean Greece, with widespread trade abroad and stable conditions at home. Then, slowly at first but with ever-increasing speed and urgency from the mid-thirteenth century onward, this settled picture begins to change. The great Peloponnesian palace complexes strengthen their defensive fortifications, building vast emergency enclosures for cattle and refugees. From about 1300 B.C. Mycenaean overseas trade begins to fall off, a decline that may have been due in large part to the piratical activities of roving bands of corsairs known as the Sea Peoples, who preyed on Mediterranean shipping lanes. More threatening still were the vast hordes of migrant tribesmen from the Eurasian steppes who began pressing across the Danube toward Anatolia and the Balkans.

It is against this background of disrupted trade routes and economic uncertainty that we must place Homer's Trojan War — a Viking-like raid carried out for the sole purpose of acquiring plunder in lieu of commerce, which is why the Greek chieftains merely sacked Troy and then sailed away again, leaving its inhabitants to reoccupy the site. Soon after 1200, a wave of barbarian nomads from Europe seems to have moved into the recently vanquished region unopposed. Similar pressure from the north soon brought down Troy's Mycenaean conquerors, whose homeland strongholds had been fatally weakened during their absence overseas. Not even a vast wall built across the Isthmus of Corinth around 1220 could hold back the invaders; they simply bypassed this obstacle by crossing the Gulf of Corinth on rafts. Modern historians speak of a Dorian invasion; myth identifies the action as the return of the sons of Heracles. Both may refer to a large force of northern Greek tribesmen led by exiled or dissident Mycenaean barons, who attacked southern Greece in several waves extending over a long period of time. Indeed, the subjugation of the Peloponnese took a full century to achieve. Among the earliest strongholds to fall, about 1200, was Nestor's Pylos, and other great Bronze Age sites ultimately suffered the same fate. The lights were going out all over the Mycenaean world, and conse-

Already credited with the unification of Attica, the quasi-legendary Athenian hero Theseus gained enduring fame by delivering Athens from the perennial threat of invasion by Minoan Crete. In mythic terms, Theseus had slain the Minotaur—an allegorical confrontation featured on the amphora at right, below. In historical terms, Mycenaean Greece had displaced Crete as the preeminent maritime power in the Aegean. Little more than a century was to pass before Mycenae found itself embroiled in another territorial war, this one with its wealthy rival Troy. The carved gem at right depicts the celebrated subterfuge that finally broke the siege of Troy: Mycenaean warriors lower themselves from the belly of the Trojan Horse, their long-sought victory all but won.

quently the period from 1100 to 750 B.C. is known, with some justice, as the Greek Dark Age.

There was, however, one striking and, as far as we know, unique exception to this melancholy chronicle of disaster: the Athenian contingent might not have distinguished itself at Troy, but Athens alone survived a hundred years of northern invasions without once surrendering. Athena's rock became a haven for aristocratic refugees, a launching point for Ionian emigration schemes, a precious cultural link between the old world and the new, and a symbol of civilization triumphant against the inroads of barbarism. It is not hard to see how old-fashioned traditionalists, at the time of Xerxes' invasion in 480 B.C., felt in a quasi-magical fashion that the Acropolis *could not* fall.

Excavation on the Acropolis shows with exceptional clarity how the threat of invasion was anticipated and successful defensive action taken against it during this period. Before 1250 a series of five interdependent terraces had been created on the north side of the rock, presumably as the foundation for a more extensive palace complex. Plato, in his *Critias*, gives what purports to be a description of this early Acropolis, and his account may, despite a liberal admixture of fantasy, contain certain facts. He says that craftsmen and farmers inhabited the area immediately below the summit, the upper part being reserved for the warrior class, who "lived in the northern section of the Acropolis, where they had constructed public dwellings and communal mess-halls for use in the winter and whatever else forms a necessary part of community life in the way of buildings for their own use and for religious purposes." It was this same warrior class that took steps to turn Athena's rock — like Mycenae, like Tiryns — into a mighty and impregnable fortress sometime after 1225. Around the entire perimeter they raised a great cyclopean wall, between three and six meters in thickness, with a tower and double gate above the western slope. The total height of the fortifications at this point was no less than 450 feet above the floor of the valley.

Peasants from the outlying districts now came flocking to Athens to seek protection in the shadow of this fortified citadel, and numerous makeshift dwellings were built on the site of the old postern stair, probably by squatters for whom there was no room inside. Meanwhile, with great ingenuity, Athens's Mycenaean engineers tackled the vital problem of obtaining a regular water supply under siege conditions — a critical consideration because the Clepsydra Spring had its source outside the walls. On the north side of the rock, however, and within the precinct, was a narrow cleft that descended some 120 feet and formed a natural well at the bottom. Eight flights of steps, the lower courses made from wooden beams, were built down this shaft — a perilous descent, judging from the number of broken waterpots found at the bottom. There seems to be little question that this dank fountain-house saved Athens from the fate that befell so many other strongholds when the threatened invasion came, and for perhaps twenty-five years provided the Acropolis with its main — often its sole — source of water. Then the danger receded, damp rotted the timbers, the lower staircase fell in, and only the upper section of the cleft, leading to the Cave of Aglauros, remained in use — and that, predictably, for ritual purposes only.

The last attempt at a Dorian take-over is tradition-

ally said to have come in 1068 B.C. with a large-scale invasion from the Peloponnese. Legend asserts that the Dorians had been promised victory by an oracle — as long as they spared Athens's ruler. Learning of this, King Codrus himself went to the enemy's camp disguised as a woodcutter and provoked some soldiers into killing him. The invasion duly failed, whereupon Athens proceeded to abolish her monarchy on the grounds that no one was worthy to succeed Codrus. Instead a group of archons, or magistrates, ruled Athens, first by appointment but after 682 as annually elected officials, a first step toward the democratic ideal. However fictional in detail, this tale may well enshrine a core of historical truth: it certainly reminds us that for three long centuries (1100–800 B.C.), while mainland Greece as a whole adjusted to the rude and poverty-stricken realities of Dorian rule, Athenians were already working out the shape of political things to come. What crystallized during the Greek Dark Age was that strange and wholly idiosyncratic entity known as the *polis,* or city-state. And as we shall see, Athens, with her unbroken traditions and her inviolate citadel, ultimately came to symbolize the *polis* in its purest, most extreme, and most ambitious form.

Fact and myth, intertwined and indistinguishable, must be taken as one by students of Attica's earliest history, for the Greeks themselves have long seen the two as inseparable. The myth of Theseus and the Minotaur, for example, remained popular well into historical times, and a full millennium after the demigod's death his legendary achievements were being perpetuated by Athenian potters. One episode in that epic tale—an encounter between Theseus and Poseidon—forms the decorative motif of the vase seen above. No less popular was the fabric of legends that surrounded the events of the Trojan War. The central band of the huge ceremonial crater at left details the story of the wedding of Peleus and the sea goddess Thetis—the union that ultimately led to the Judgment of Paris, which in turn ignited the war. That ten-year siege, which was marked by bitter and inconclusive combat, is the subject of the oldest surviving illustrated Greek book, a fragment of which is reproduced at upper left.

II
TIME
OF
TURMOIL

Nothing so clearly indicates the authoritarian, elitist nature of Mycenaean culture as its total collapse at the time of the Dorian invasions. The presence of so many warrior chiefs at Troy unquestionably encouraged would-be usurpers at home as well as abroad, and legend has it that while Agamemnon fought on the windy plain below Priam's citadel, the Greek monarch's cousin was seducing his wife, Clytemnaestra, in the great mainland fortress of Mycenae. When Troy finally fell after ten long years of warfare and siege, the Greeks at once set out for home. Many perished on the journey, and few of those who reached their destination found things quite as they had been before. Agamemnon was murdered by Clytemnaestra and her lover, and Odysseus was obliged to clear his palace of local barons who were living off the royal estate and courting his wife, Penelope. Domestically, Greece was suffering the usual weakening effects of a long overseas campaign. Internecine feuding made these Mycenaean strongholds still more vulnerable, and within a generation the Dorians struck. In not much more than a century the old fortresses all fell, centralized government broke down, and the Greek mainland reverted to local subsistence farming in harsh, impoverished conditions. The feudal system lingered on, but only at the parochial or manorial level, a ghost of its former self.

Athens survived this change of regime without ever succumbing to a direct assault. Her inhabitants kept up some semblance of civilization, even of luxury — as the recently discovered tomb of a wealthy Athenian lady who died in the mid-ninth century makes clear. Her coffin, which is adorned with models of granaries — possibly to suggest the source of her husband's wealth

— contained gold filigree jewelry, glass and faience beads, and ivory stamp seals, indicating that by 850 B.C. local craftsmanship had recovered and overseas trade was once again picking up. But the previous two centuries had witnessed a cultural recession even in Athens. Her potters, no more immune to localism than anyone else, broke away from Mycenaean influence and began to develop long-ignored motifs based on traditional peasant designs. This new line of ceramics, called Geometric because of a preponderance of abstract patterns, proved extraordinarily popular and soon spread across the entire Aegean, carried by successive waves of Mycenaean immigrants. Many of these colonists settled on the Anatolian coast, in the area that was known to the ancient Greeks as Ionia.

The later intellectual preeminence of both Athens and Ionia may well have been due to the fact that they offered refuge to cultured Mycenaeans during the great invasions. Athens's position as an unconquered stronghold explains why many old traditions survived there but nowhere else. Epic poetry, for example, was carried across the Aegean by bands of Mycenaean exiles and achieved its last and finest flowering in the eighth century, when Homer drew on this age-old material to fashion two masterpieces, the *Iliad* and the *Odyssey*.

Soon after 750 B.C. a true alphabet came into use in the Aegean world, a development that was to have a far-reaching impact upon the course of Western civilization. Among other things, the evolution of written law codes made the terms of justice available to all men on an equal basis, rather than leaving them dependent upon the whim of some lord. The mid-eighth century also witnessed the dawn of recorded history, the genesis of Archaic Greek art, and the great diaspora of Greek adventurers and colonists that over the next several centuries established Hellenic outposts on every littoral from the Black Sea to the Straits of Gibraltar.

By the 440's Herodotus could write of "our common language, the altars and sacrifices of which we all partake, the common character which we all bear." Yet paradoxically, this intangible notion of "Greekness" had its genesis during the Dark Age, a period of apparent eclipse. Perhaps "gestation" better describes the process, for after the great twelfth-century invasions, the Balkan peninsula was temporarily cut off from outside cultural influences — Oriental, Egyptian, and Western. The Aegean basin became, for all intents and purposes, a Greek lake framed by a natural ring of small coastal communities.

By about 800 B.C. this geographical unit had achieved a recognizable cultural identity. Its variant dialects all stemmed from a common language, and its gods and goddesses all belonged to the same basic pantheon. Politically, however, a stubborn separatism prevailed. Ubiquitous mountain ranges and grim winters made for poor communications, and natural cantons discouraged federalism. The protection once offered by the great overlord in his cyclopean fortress had disappeared forever, along with the inefficient bureaucracy of scribes. Yet the system did not change in essence; it merely shrank. Throughout the Dark Age each village still clustered around a "big house," or *oikos,* owned by some local feudal baron and more often than not set on a defensive outcrop. In return for the villagers' services and tithes, the lord gave them military protection when danger threatened. He was, in fact, a warrior-landlord with a retinue of armed servants, presiding over a debased, poverty-stricken version of the Mycenaean society it had supplanted.

By the end of the eighth century this system of government was already under heavy fire. Accusations of gross venality and injustice abounded. The abolition of kingship had been a beginning, even though this, like the signing of Magna Charta at Runnymede, was primarily a move by the barons to secure more power for themselves. Nor had anyone yet conceived a viable alternative to rule by "the best"; that alternative did not emerge for another two centuries. Nevertheless, many felt that reform of traditional arbitrary privileges was long overdue. This trend drew strength from the emergence of a new potential power bloc whose capital derived from trade rather than from landed property. Some of these men were self-made, others aristocrats who as yet lacked entrée into the charmed circle of power. What they all had in common was political ambition which could find no legitimate outlet in the existing system. The emergence of a collective *polis* ideal, combined with grim hardship and injustice among the depressed agricultural population, gave these people precisely the opening — and the support — that they needed. Laws alone, especially those framed by and for the ruling class, could neither alleviate distress nor solve economic problems. Something else had to be tried, and the emergence, soon after 700 B.C., of the hoplite phalanx seemed to point the way to it.

The hoplite phalanx was a citizen levy of foot soldiers, a well-trained, well-organized body armed with spears, shields, helmets, corslets, greaves, and short swords. Its members included farmers, traders, crafts-men, and aristocrats who could not afford service with the cavalry. The phalanx fought as a unit, shoulder to shoulder in defense of the *polis,* with each man's shield protecting his neighbor's flank. A more effective social leveler could hardly be imagined, for the sole criterion for enrollment was the ability to purchase a hoplite's armor, which increasing numbers of citizens could now afford to do. This military reorganization led, not illogically, to a fresh assessment of citizens in terms of their capital resources rather than their birth — a momentous development. In every way the phalanx struck a deadly blow at the old privileged warrior aristocracy. The latter's protection was no longer indispensable; the people had learned to shift for themselves, and as a result the whole concept of warfare underwent a radical change. It did not take long for the citizens of Athens to realize that the phalanx was also a potential weapon of enormous power in the coming political struggle, a counterweight to any dictatorial baron's private army.

In short, Athenian society was ripe for an age of coups d'etat — armed take-over bids by various opposition leaders who could count on popular support. Between roughly 650 and 550 B.C. a whole crop of such usurpers sprang up in the Greek world. They were known as *tyrannoi* — hence our word "tyrant." Gyges of Lydia set the trend: once his usurpation had been approved by the Delphic Oracle — a gesture that in effect gave the principle of tyranny divine endorsement — numerous aspirants made their own bids for power, many of them successfully. *Tyrannoi* were not, by and large, unpopular, since they cashed in on public grievances to seize and hold power. They busied themselves with economic and agricultural reforms, public works

programs, and the energetic promotion of overseas trade. And they deliberately courted mass support, upon which they could rely as long as they continued to provide goods and services.

Athens had been less affected by these developments than other Greek cities, however. The early unification of Attica had left her, for the time being, with adequate territorial resources. By the mid-seventh century her agricultural position was grim, but it had not yet become impossible. The indiscriminate export of farm produce, grain in particular, by wealthy landowners anxious to purchase foreign luxury goods had created shortages on the home market. Attica's population had not yet grown to the point where famine was an immediate threat, but many improvident smallholders had borrowed recklessly on the security of their persons, failed to repay those loans, and become de facto serfs to their creditors. Some were even sold into slavery overseas. As landowners increasingly sought liquid capital rather than chattels, this practice became alarmingly frequent.

The potential dangers of such a situation hardly need emphasizing. Formerly free men with nothing but servitude of one sort or another to look forward to would surely throw in their lot with any rebel leader who promised them a fresh start — or so many would-be *tyrannoi* must have argued. But when such an attempt was first made — around 632 B.C. — it proved an embarrassing failure. Economically, Athens had lagged behind the times; not for another half century would conditions grow bad enough to bring her farm laborers to the revolutionary boil. This premature coup nevertheless has particular interest for us, since it is the first — though by no means the last — occasion in Athens's recorded history on which the Acropolis and its shrines play a dramatic role.

At the time of Cylon's attempted take-over, Athena's rock had not yet acquired those splendid architectural adornments that we most closely associate with it. It was still a fortress with a grim, cyclopean enceinte. At the western entrance, fortification walls and guard towers stood where the Propylaea would later gleam in the clear Attic air. Marble, in fact, was conspicuous by its absence, and neither the Parthenon nor its sixth-century predecessor yet existed. Such buildings as stood on the rock were made of mud brick and terra-cotta, perishable materials that suffered badly during the subsequent Persian sack of Athens. But in some shape or form a cluster of shrines — that of Athena Polias above all — undoubtedly occupied the old traditional site near the northern edge of the rock, the spot where Poseidon's trident mark and saline spring, together with the olive tree of Athena, marked a cult center that dated back to the rock's first human habitation. Here was housed the goddess's archaic wooden image and, a little to the southeast, her great open-air altar.

Like many early Greek revolutionaries, Cylon came from an aristocratic family. He was extraordinarily good-looking, and he had also proven himself to be a distinguished athlete, winning the footrace at Olympia in 640 B.C. Young, handsome, tough, wealthy, and glamorous, Cylon obviously possessed many of the qualities essential for a would-be *tyrannos*. Nor can there be any doubt regarding his ambitions: he married the daughter of Theagenes, the *tyrannos* of nearby Megara. Promised the help of Megarian troops by his

father-in-law, Cylon took the further precaution of
consulting the Delphic Oracle as to the advisability of
staging a coup. He was told to seize the Acropolis "at
the greatest festival of Zeus." Cylon, a far from modest
man, at once assumed this must mean the famous
festival of Olympia, where he himself had won glory
as an athlete. But — as the Oracle well knew — there
were other possible interpretations. The Athenians
themselves, for instance, celebrated a great feast of
Zeus known as the Diasia. Cylon had made up his mind,
however, and he planned his attack for August, to
coincide with the Olympic Games — a time when some
of his more formidable aristocratic opponents might
well be out of town.

Cylon seems to have been as stupid as he was ego-
tistical, a combination that foredoomed his coup. It
apparently never occurred to him, for example, that
the people would not at once rally to his cause, and
how far he ever bothered to sound out their feelings
is uncertain. His decision to employ Megarian troops
was a bad psychological blunder as well, for the
Athenians would not be slow to deduce that Cylon's
father-in-law meant to grab Attica as part of his own
fief. This brought *polis* patriotism into the affair,
obscuring the idea of agrarian revolution. In addition,
why should the peasantry trouble to exchange one
aristocratic government for another? As a result, the
first part of the coup went off as planned, but its second
stage simply collapsed. Cylon, accompanied by Theagenes's troops and a group of his own young friends,
seized the Acropolis in broad daylight — another
blunder, since many potential supporters of the coup
worked in the fields all day. The rebels probably

ascended the rock by the old steps on the north face
and surprised the sentinels at the Postern Gate. Even
then their troubles were not over, for Herodotus states
that they failed to capture the entire Acropolis — and
the well-guarded area that held out against them contained the rock's only water supply. They had, moreover, failed to bring food with them, and consequently
their position was untenable from the very beginning.

Nevertheless, with a characteristic mixture of bra-
vado and foolhardiness, Cylon proclaimed himself ruler
of Athens and called upon the populace to join him.
The Athenian people quickly sized up the situation —
and sat tight. Furthermore, the city's magistrates —
whom Cylon had not bothered to neutralize — took
prompt and effective counteraction. Messengers sped
out to the surrounding countryside, where local bosses
lost little time in mustering their citizen levies. Far from
striking a blow for liberty, the field workers obediently
shouldered their mattocks, marched into town, and
threw a siege cordon around the Acropolis. After a day
or two it became clear that Cylon and his supporters
were in a hopeless position anyway, and most of the
peasants drifted back to their fields, where more pressing tasks awaited. Before leaving they authorized the
archons to deal with the matter in any way they saw fit.

The solution was obvious if prosaic: block all exits
from the Acropolis, deprive Cylon and his men of food
and water, and let the burning August sun do the rest.
The chief archon, Megacles the Alcmaeonid, settled
down to starve the would-be revolutionaries into surrender. The besieged apparently sought sanctuary in
the immediate vicinity of Athena's altar and temple,
and one charge later leveled against Cylon was that he

despoiled the shrine of its treasures. If he did so, it was in order to bribe his way through the cordon under cover of darkness, since one morning the desperate little band found their leader and his brother gone. (No one knows what became of Cylon after his escape; some sources say he suffered the same fate as his followers.) Megacles then decided that the time had come to act. The defenders were half dead of thirst — and if any of them did die in the sanctuary, holy ground would be polluted, a serious matter. He therefore invited the survivors to come down and stand fair trial before the Areopagus Council. He promised them they would not suffer the death penalty, nor any bodily harm.

The desperate men wavered, then finally accepted Megacles's terms. They took lengths of braided cord — perhaps from the temple hangings — and knotted them together to form a long rope. They attached one end to Athena's image, the holy olive-wood totem; clinging to the other end, they marched down from the Acropolis, thus keeping themselves technically in sanctuary. Parched and unkempt, the remnants of Cylon's forces stumbled out through the Enneapylon, descended the ramp, and turned north toward the old marketplace, playing out the cord as they went. As they neared their destination, however, the rope snapped — "of its own accord," according to Herodotus, which suggests that some people assumed otherwise. Megacles's immediate reaction must certainly have lent color to such a suspicion, for he cried out that this was a sign that the goddess had rejected these impious wretches as suppliants. His men rushed to seize the hapless revolutionaries. Some were stoned to death by the mob while others

were torn from the nearby Altar of the Furies, where they had fled for sanctuary, and butchered in cold blood. One or two, with special presence of mind, clung to the archons' wives, and so managed to escape unscathed.

As a result of this scandalous incident Megacles's family, the powerful Alcmaeonid clan, was put under a curse and exiled from Attica — although they seem to have returned and become active in politics again before many more years were out. What Cylon's coup reveals is a fierce internecine struggle between rival aristocratic clans whose leaders would stop at nothing to eliminate their opponents. The only direct political concession made as a result of this episode was the publication of a revision of Athens's law code. That revision was drawn up in 620 B.C. by Draco, who made the death penalty so common that citizens said his laws were written in blood, not ink. But repressive measures proved no substitute for long-term reform, and all our evidence suggests that during the period between 620 and 570 B.C. matters came rapidly to a crisis. These years saw the incorporation of Eleusis into Attica, local wars for the possession of nearby Salamis, and — perhaps most significant — the removal of the Agora from its old home by the Areopagus to the new, less central site that it was to occupy throughout classical antiquity. This area was a rough triangle with its base on the line of the Enneakrounos conduit head and its apex at the point where the Sacred Way from Eleusis converged on the roads to Acharnae and Piraeus. Burials in this area, hitherto frequent, were now discontinued. Instead tombs were built along the avenues leading away from the city. The general picture suggests a sharp rise in

The gradual democratization of ancient Greece was given renewed impetus in the seventh century B.C. by the formation of the hoplite phalanx, a citizen army raised to defend the city-state against its adversaries, both foreign and domestic. Any man who could afford to purchase a hoplite's armor was automatically enrolled, regardless of his social rank. Within a relatively short space of time this urban militia—depicted in full regalia on the vase detail below—had become a significant political force.

the city's population, and the need — both at home and abroad — for substantially more living space.

Nevertheless, the ruling aristocracy continued intransigent and the plight of smallholders worsened. A time came when authoritarianism evoked not conformist obedience, but threats of bloody revolution and a call for forcible redistribution of the land. Eventually both sides agreed to call in an arbitrator with extraordinary powers to completely overhaul the constitution. The man chosen was Solon, a merchant-aristocrat who somehow convinced both sides that he had their special interests at heart. Solon cut the Gordian knot of the agrarian dilemma by canceling all land debts outright and pulling up the mortgage stones that recorded them. No free citizen could ever again contract loans on the security of his person, or suffer imprisonment for debt — a record unequaled by many European countries until the mid-nineteenth century — and those who had been enslaved were bought back. Land was not redistributed, but the export of all produce except oil was made illegal — a clear attack on agricultural profiteers. Attica, as Solon well knew, lacked raw materials apart from clay and marble. To help compensate for this, he decreed that every father must teach his son a trade. In particular, he encouraged the development of fine pottery, offering citizenship on advantageous terms to any foreign craftsman who would settle in Athens. This policy proved so successful that by 550 B.C. Athenian pottery began to eclipse that of Corinth, which had previously monopolized the market.

Solon also seems to have initiated a noteworthy building program. To this period archaeologists assign a new council chamber, a shrine on the Athena Nike

The year 632 brought the first of a succession of coups d'etat that were to become a feature of seventh-century Athenian politics. Led by a handsome, ambitious, and foolhardy young athlete named Cylon, a band of dissident aristocrats seized the Acropolis and brazenly proclaimed themselves the rightful rulers of Athens. However, the popular support that the rebels had counted on never materialized. Instead, the loyal hoplites threw a siege cordon around the citadel. Under Megacles's supervision, the rebels were slowly starved into submission—and when they finally surrendered, the archon had them slain. For his Draconian tactics, Megacles was briefly exiled from Athens. Recalled some years later, he died forgiven—and the grateful citizens of Athens erected the gently tapering funeral stele at left in his honor.

bastion, and, in all likelihood, the temple known as the Hecatompedon, or "Hundred-footer," that stood upon the future site of the Parthenon. It was also in about 570 B.C. that Athenian coinage made its first appearance, a sure sign of rising prosperity. We may assume that these developments were all related, and in fact represented the civic and religious propaganda that was an integral part of Solon's policy for Athens. Indeed, in his surviving poetry Solon portrays Pallas Athena as both Zeus' favorite daughter and the city of Athens's special guardian. This Pallas, the warrior-maiden and patroness of the arts, contrasts sharply with the archaic Athena whose olive-wood totem stood in the old temple on the north side of the Acropolis. It was Pallas the warrior-virgin on whom political leaders from Solon to Pericles concentrated their attention. They saw her as the symbolic embodiment of all Athens's civic, imperial, and even intellectual aspirations, the focal point for all ceremony during Attica's greatest festival, the Panathenaea. And it was in her honor that the Parthenon itself arose during Athens's finest hour, the Age of Pericles.

After announcing his reforms, Solon wisely went abroad for ten years. Economically, the new system proved a resounding success, but increased affluence gave more people time to play at politics, and the result was internecine chaos. Solon might have avoided an immediate crisis, but he had done nothing to break up the old local clans. Three main factions now emerged: the men of the plain, the coast, and the hills, the last led by Solon's kinsman Pisistratus. After a decade of violent political infighting and anarchy, Pisistratus came to the conclusion that political order could best be restored under a dictatorship, with himself as sole ruler. Solon, who had by this time returned to Athens, guessed the would-be usurper's plans and warned the people against him, but without success. In 561 Pisistratus tricked the Assembly into granting him an armed bodyguard, and, then, following Cylon's example, seized the Acropolis, a sine qua non — symbolically as well as practically — for any usurper.

Not that Pisistratus's position, at least initially, was all that secure. He twice found himself thrown out of office by rival aristocratic juntas, and on the second occasion he was forced to spend some years in exile. By 546, however, he was back once again, this time with a private army and plentiful cash reserves. The formula proved irresistible. Long-term loans to small farmers, plus the redistribution of his enemies' confiscated estates, made Pisistratus surprisingly popular; Athenians afterwards looked back on his reign as a golden age. When he died in 527 his sons, Hippias and Hipparchus, took over the government unopposed and enjoyed a political honeymoon with the various opposition clans, whose leaders all seem to have held office during this period. It was, paradoxically, the years of Pisistratid dictatorship that saw Athens cease to be a mere country village and begin to take shape as the gleaming, violet-crowned citadel that we associate, first and foremost, with the Periclean Age.

Pisistratus, who had long appreciated the value of Solon's civic propaganda, began to adopt similar methods at a very early stage in his career. Several years before his first coup, he either instituted or greatly embellished the special quadrennial festival known as the Greater Panathenaea. It is at this point that organized

Having resolved Athens's grave constitutional crisis of 594 in a manner that was to satisfy laborers and landowners alike, the merchant-aristocrat Solon turned his attention to civic beautification. Under his aegis shrines were erected on the Acropolis to celebrate a new embodiment of Athena. Solon saw the goddess as a warrior-maiden, and this vision of her was glorified at Attica's greatest annual festival, the Panathenaea. Time and abuse have reduced the Panathenaic Way to impassable cobbles (right), but in the 550's the path was well paved and celebrants could follow it from the gates of the city to the foot of the Acropolis itself. The amphora at left shows Athena the warrior-maiden awarding prizes at the Panathenaic games.

competitions in horse racing, athletics, and music appear as part of the festival, with beautiful oil-filled Attic amphoras given as prizes. Perhaps the best-known part of this festival, immortalized on the Parthenon frieze, is the splendid spectacle of the Panathenaic procession. To celebrate Athena's birth, which traditionally fell at the beginning of August, there was an all-night ceremony with dancing and a race in which all the contestants carried torches. At dawn on the following morning, the procession formed at the Dipylon Gate, while spectators crowded into the grandstands along the Panathenaic Way. The object of the procession was to escort a new robe for Athena's olive-wood image to her shrine on the Acropolis. The route taken lay southeast through the Agora, after which it skirted around the Eleusinion and the Prytaneion, making for the western approach to the Acropolis. Oddly enough, the robe, which had scenes from the battle of the gods and giants woven into it, was drawn as far as the Areopagus on a wheeled ship, draped from the ship's mast like a sail. For the last uphill stage of its journey, through the Propylaea, it was borne by Athenian maidens. The frieze gives us a most vivid picture of this procession, with marshals and sacrificial victims, musicians and pitcher-bearers, aristocratic maidens with their baskets, resident aliens wearing purple robes and holding dishes of sacrificial cakes, old men with olive branches and — in pride of place — the dashing, supercilious young riders of Athens's elite cavalry corps. Clearly one object of this reorganized Panathenaea, with its emphasis on public athletics, was to set Athens up in competition with those other, more internationally famous centers, Olympia and Delphi.

Later, when his position was secure, Pisistratus embarked on a vast program of cultural, religious, and economic reform, all emphasizing the same fundamental principles: the glorification of Athens under Athena, work and uplift for the citizenry, and the bedazzlement of country peasants and foreign visitors alike. Every *tyrannos* envisaged such a program — Pisistratus simply undertook it on a larger and more ambitious scale than most. In doing so he never forgot that propaganda and public works schemes cost money. He levied a flat 10 per cent tax on agricultural produce, derived a sizable income from mining investments in Thrace, and did much to exploit Attica's own extensive silver deposits at Laurium. With the resultant capital he improved drainage and harbor facilities and enlarged Athens's water supply, installing a new public fountain at the southeast corner of the Agora.

Aristotle suggests that the chief motive for such civic construction work was to reduce unemployment and keep the urban proletariat out of political mischief — and there is no question that Pisistratus spent massive sums of money on projects from which he derived no direct or immediate return. These projects included the construction of at least two temples and the reorganization, on a centralized basis, of Attica's chief rural festivals. Both programs contain more than a hint of opium for the masses, but both also express the symbolic identification not only of Athena with Athens but also of Athens with Attica. Pisistratus knew very well that the gods of grain and grape could not be ignored by any leader whose position depended on popular backing and economic prosperity, and he therefore placated Demeter of Eleusis by building the first hall for her Mysteries. The old country festival of Dionysus was given a new home — and a new look — in Athens..

Pisistratus also seems to have been the first Athenian leader who saw the potential of art and literature not merely as a vehicle for exploiting religious or patriotic sentiment after Solon's manner but as a public cultural utility. Pisistratus may not have commissioned an official recension of the *Iliad* and *Odyssey,* as scholars once believed, but his son Hipparchus did decree that complete recitations of Homer were to be given by professional bards at the Panathenaea festival. Pisistratus encouraged what had hitherto been little more than a rough mime, with song and recitative, during the Dionysiac festival. The result, introduced at the festival in 534, was what may fairly be termed the first Greek tragedy. In this innovation, traditionally ascribed to the poet Thespis, one voice was distinct from, and often addressed to, the singing chorus. State-organized competitions in both tragedy and comedy soon followed.

All these innovations were enhanced by an architecturally ambitious building program. Pisistratus planned a gigantic and frankly ostentatious temple to replace the old shrine of Olympian Zeus that stood southeast of the Acropolis, but after the expulsion of his son Hippias the scheme was discontinued. (It is no accident that the two rulers who carried this tasteless monstrosity to completion — Antiochus Epiphanes and the emperor Hadrian — were both, like Pisistratus himself, unalloyed autocrats.) At this same time Pisistratus either rebuilt, or adorned with a peristyle and sculptures, what is known as the Old Temple of Athena. This was a Doric edifice situated just south of the Erechtheum. The representation on its east pediment of the battle between gods and giants — reason overcoming brute force — may be taken as a characteristic Pisistratid contribution to the new Athenian mythology.

Athens's fifth-century cultural background was now almost complete. One element still hung fire, however, as under a dictatorship it must, and that was the political concept of freedom. With Pisistratus's accession to power, democratic notions had been shunted aside while Athens found her cultural identity and worked hard to achieve some sort of economic margin. Affluence had in fact underwritten the Pisistratid regime from start to finish, and when Persian activities in Thrace and the Hellespont brought about a trade recession it was Pisistratus's sons, Hippias and Hipparchus, who felt the winds of change. The Alcmaeonidae, exiled once again for subversive activities, were plotting a comeback under their leader Cleisthenes. To this end they angled — successfully in the end — for Spartan cooperation, and they also got the endorsement of the Delphic Oracle, whose fire-ravaged temple they had rebuilt with lavish marble facing. In 514 Hipparchus was assassinated, whereupon the Alcmaeonidae made two unsuccessful attempts to dislodge Hippias by force. During the second of these attempts, a Spartan admiral was killed, national prestige became involved, and in 510 Cleomenes I of Sparta took to the field in person. Hippias barricaded himself on the Acropolis, but he was forced to surrender when the Athenians caught his whole family trying to slip across the frontier of Attica. Cleomenes, having intervened officially to restore freedom, had no option but to go home and pray that his Athenian friends would eventually come out on top.

For two years, Athens witnessed a ferocious struggle between the followers of Cleisthenes and the pro-Spartan supporters of Isagoras. In 508 Isagoras won the archonship, and Cleisthenes decided to make a final, desperate appeal to the people. Those who revere him as the founding father of Athenian democracy might do well to ponder how late in the day he saw the light. What he apparently did was to force a measure through the Assembly, over Isagoras's head, that enfranchised free citizens regardless of property qualifications. Thus, in one stroke, he acquired a devoted political clique that could always outvote his opponents. Isagoras, in panic, appealed to Sparta. Cleomenes marched on Athens, where with typical Spartan arrogance he made two fatal errors. He ordered the exile of no less than seven hundred "unreliable" families, the Alcmaeonidae included, and he proclaimed the dissolution of Solon's quasi-democratic Council of Four Hundred, replacing it with a caucus of yes-men, followers of Isagoras. At this point the Athenians took action. The violent overthrow of elected government, coming so soon after Hippias's ejection, was bad enough; a reversion to aristocratic oligarchy backed by foreign troops was intolerable. The Assembly refused to budge; Cleomenes threatened; and then, without warning, a violent riot broke out. Isagoras and his Spartan friends found themselves forced to seek refuge on Athena's rock — where, after two days without food or water, they laid down their arms in return for safe conduct out of the city. The moral victory was complete: a Spartan king had been humiliated and the principle of free government upheld. Cleisthenes was recalled from exile in triumph. Athenian democracy had at last come of age.

"For surely shall I win first prize, and bring it to my home," a self-confident athlete declares in the Iliad. *Had that athlete's performance matched his high expectations, Homer's braggart would have won an oil-filled amphora like the one at right, which depicts a footrace held during the Panathenaic festival. The graceful statuette below, whose hollow torso once held rubdown oil, may also have been an athletic award, for the tiny figure mimes an athlete in his moment of triumph as he ties a fillet, or victory band, across his brow.*

III

THE BULWARK OF HELLAS

In 507 B.C. Athens became a democracy once more, and the Acropolis henceforth housed only the goddess and her priests. Except in special emergencies, human aspirants for power remained below. "Nothing too much," intoned the Delphic Oracle; man must not aspire to equal the gods. The concept of Athena as both warrior-maiden and guardian totem might denote separate aspects of one deity — might even hint at a social split between the few and the many — but she stood above mere political factions. She was as popular with the democracy as she had been with the tyrants. It is possible — although fiercely disputed — that some sort of temple stood on the site of the Parthenon as early as Pisistratus's day, but the full development of Pallas Athena's civic and municipal characteristics belonged to Cleisthenes and his successors.

A song from the period just after the fall of the last tyrant calls upon Pallas Athena and Zeus, her father, to "sustain this city and its citizens without suffering and civil strife and untimely deaths." Clearly it was time for an end to internal squabbling, and the construction of new municipal buildings — including a council chamber and a place of assembly on the hill known as the Pnyx — symbolized Athens's hard-won civic concord. The Agora was conceived of for the first time as an overall architectural complex, an embodiment of the new egalitarianism. The Oracle's intervention was piously rewarded with a magnificent treasury, built in Delphi to house Athenian offerings.

The most significant action undertaken by Cleisthenes's new regime was not the initiation of building projects, however, but the dispatch of an embassy to seek some sort of accommodation with Persia. For while sixth-century Athens had been working out her own political and economic problems in parochial isolation, other developments — just as far-reaching, and more immediately consequential — had been taking place on the eastern side of the Aegean. In the cities of Ionia, for example, a new and scintillating intellectual climate had emerged, with thinkers and scientists making rational breakthroughs today referred to as the "Greek miracle." Yet it was not so much this bright Ionian littoral that concerned the mainland Greeks as the vast and alien power brooding behind it. The meteoric rise of Persia as an imperial power seems to have taken the entire eastern Mediterranean by surprise. In 550, the Near East was still a conglomeration of small, local principalities; twenty-five years later, Persia had absorbed them all, emerging under her dynamic leader Cyrus the Great as the largest single empire the ancient world had ever seen.

For the Greeks, Cyrus's most alarming achievement — certainly the one which brought the Persian threat home to them as nothing else could have done — was his victory over that proud and wealthy monarch, Croesus of Lydia, in 546. The Ionian cities now came under the rule of Persian provincial governors, or satraps. (A number of Ionian artists and intellectuals, among them Pythagoras, chose to emigrate rather than live without true independence, and some of them eventually reached Athens.) Initially, the Persians left their Greek subjects alone; they even seem to have given Ionian merchants certain laissez-faire privileges. The accession of Darius I in 521 changed this accommodating picture, however, for Darius taxed his provinces — Ionia included — with ruthless, but economic-

ally wrongheaded, thoroughness. Not content with exploring the trade routes to India, he also sought to expand into Europe. The expedition he led across the Danube in 514 was carried out with Ionian Greek assistance, and it left Persia firmly in control of Thrace and the Hellespont.

Consequently, the new and rather shaky Athenian democratic regime had every reason for trying to reach an accommodation with Persia — if only as a temporizing measure. One particularly urgent motive was provided by Hippias, the banished Pisistratid tyrant, who had set up an alternative government-in-exile and was energetically bidding for Persian support. For nearly a decade both sides plagued Darius with rival embassies. About 500, Persia finally decided in favor of Hippias, and this move, combined with Darius's tough fiscal policy and ever-expanding ambitions, drove the Ionian Greeks to attempt a large-scale revolt. The rising was well planned, and it gained a number of initial successes. However, common military action over a period of years had never been a Greek forte, and the Persians, with methodical patience, proceeded to reduce their rebellious subjects piecemeal by using the divide-and-conquer principle. It took them six years to achieve their goal, but with the fall of the rebels' main stronghold in 494 the Ionian revolt was finally over.

The failure of the Ionian rebellion had various consequences, of which the most immediate — and indeed the most important — was that it made a Persian invasion of mainland Greece inevitable. At the beginning of the revolt, Athens had been talked into sending a twenty-ship squadron to support the Ionian cause. There were some hopeful early victories, one of which

Athenian leaders of the late sixth century were to popularize the concept of Athena as Nike, the goddess of victory, ignoring the gentler virtues long associated with the rough-hewn wooden totem, known as the xoanon, that had been the focus of the guardian goddess's cult for centuries. Although she was the daughter of Zeus (left) and the niece of Poseidon, Athena lacked the extraordinary powers of either. Her gifts were of a more mundane sort, which made her an increasingly curious protectress of an increasingly bellicose city-state. Athenians subscribed to the myth that Athena had sprung fully formed from her father's brow—a miraculous event recorded on the amphora below—and they credited Zeus' daughter with having invented musical instruments, farm implements, and cooking utensils. It is this prosaic, irenic Athena who flies her owl at right.

was commemorated by the construction of a new temple on Cape Sunium. In 498, a combined Athenian and Ionian force burned the Persian provincial capital of Sardis, but this act provoked swift reprisals, and from then on the tide turned against the rebels. Seeing this, the Athenians recalled their squadron and took no further part in the war. They even went so far, in 496, as to elect an archon of strong Pisistratid sympathies. But the burning of Sardis remained an affront that Darius could not tolerate and would not forget. Whenever he sat down to dinner, a slave was commanded to murmur in his ear: "Sire, remember the Athenians." The reminder was symbolic rather than practical; Darius never forgot an injury.

One Athenian who clearly saw the writing on the wall was the young, brilliant, and pugnacious politician Themistocles, elected archon for the critical year of 493. Under his inspiration and guidance, work began on developing the natural harbor of Piraeus, which was soon to become Athens's port and navy yard. A Persian invasion fleet set sail for Athens in 492, but an opportune storm wrecked the armada and gave the Athenians a couple of years' respite. However, in the summer of 490 two of Darius's top commanders, Datis and Artaphernes, sailed across the Aegean with a large task force and landed at Marathon Bay, some twenty-three miles northeast of Athens. With them, as guide and liaison officer, came old Hippias, Pisistratus's son, who hoped to regain the position of supreme power from which he had been so ignominiously ousted twenty years earlier. A group of influential Athenians, led by the Alcmaeonid clan, was in private communication with the invaders as they advanced.

Like others before them, this group of would-be usurpers badly underestimated the capacity of Athenian individualists to take effective, concerted action when danger threatened the *polis*. After an inevitable round of bickering and argument, the Assembly voted to "take provisions and march"; the city's hoplites were to contain the Persian beachhead at Marathon before an attack on the city could develop. The subsequent action — in which 9,000 Athenians defeated a vastly superior Persian army and then force marched back to Athens to stave off the threat of a seaborne invasion — is a justly famous episode in European history. Miltiades, the commander whose strategy won the day, became an overnight hero. The first round in the Athenian-Persian conflict had been won, and won decisively, by Athens alone. The Spartans, who arrived after the battle was over, had no option but to congratulate the victors and march back home.

The psychological impact of Marathon was enormous. For the first time a Greek hoplite force had beaten the Persians in the field — something the Ionians, in six years of revolt, had never contrived to do. Few Athenians appreciated that all they had won was a respite, however — that the Persian threat had been stood off, not eliminated. (Among the few was Themistocles, who once again found himself holding an unpopular opinion that later proved to be embarrassingly correct.) The immediate effect of the victory was to boost the collective Athenian psyche, and that optimism found expression in a rash of building activity on the Acropolis. New stone quarries were opened on Mount Pentelicus, a few miles outside Athens, which from then on provided the city with a seemingly inexhaustible supply of fine white marble. During the ensuing decade, forerunners of both the Parthenon and the Propylaea — Mnesicles's vast, ornamental western gateway — were begun. Only the Persian invasion of 480, culminating in the sack of Athens, prevented their completion; the massive foundations that were laid for the Older Parthenon still underpin its more famous successor.

The Old Propylon, a comparatively modest venture, was probably complete by the time of the Persian attack, although its stonework remained undressed. It was thus the first construction of Pentelic marble to adorn the Acropolis. Little of it remains — some blocks and steps, part of a pilaster, slabs that formed the backing for a bench — but its general structure can be deduced with some confidence. It was little more than a porch with four Doric columns on either side of the wall gateways, and its alignment was more southwest-northeast than that of the later structure. Outside the Propylon was a forecourt, perhaps hexagonal, around which ran a marble bench surmounted by a dado. Above the uppermost stone course of the wall itself there were further courses of mud brick, reinforced by stout upright posts with two-by-four slats nailed across them.

That the Older Parthenon was a conscious and deliberate commemoration of the victory over the Persians at Marathon there can be little doubt. For one thing, the temple's plans were set forth in 489, during the archonship of Aristides the Just, who had played a distinguished role in the battle of Marathon. Building was officially begun at the Panathenaic festival of 488 — on August 31, when the rising sun shone straight along the line of the proposed temple's axis. It is likely, although

Led by the warrior-king Cyrus, sixth-century Persia evolved into the mightiest empire the world had ever seen. Lydia fell under Persian sway in 546, and Ionian Greece followed roughly six years later. Mainland Greece—seen at left in the map below—braced for the inevitable invasion, which came in 490. Guided by the charismatic and fearless Miltiades, a vastly outnumbered Athenian army succeeded in turning back the Persians at Marathon. That stunning—and falsely reassuring—victory was subsequently celebrated in popular song, public works, and special coinage. The ten-drachma piece seen in obverse and reverse at left is said to commemorate an Athenian triumph over Persian invaders.

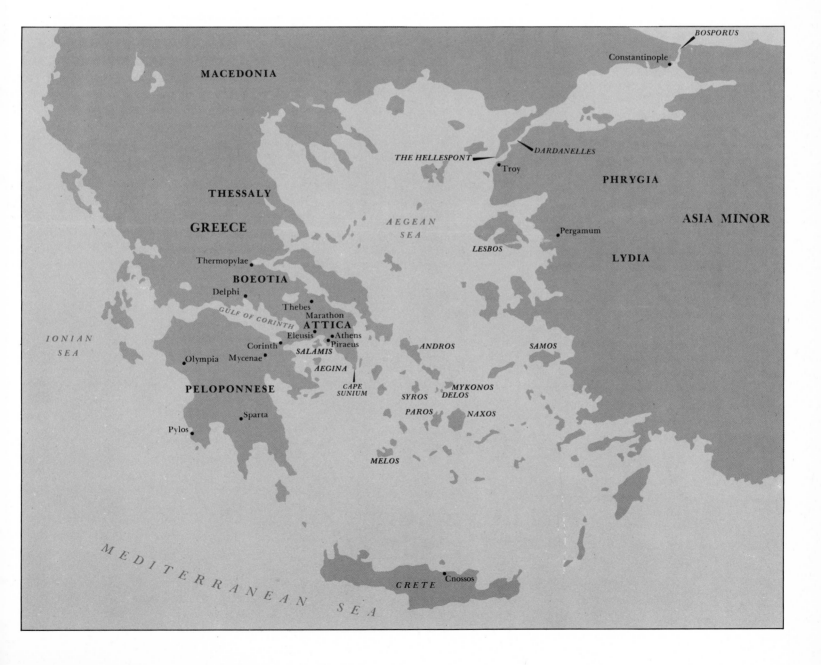

not certain, that a much smaller shrine already stood
on this site, one to which we can attribute various
pieces of surviving decorative material — lions and
snakes, a cornice incised with flying birds, and a blue-
bearded trinity that may conceivably represent Cecrops,
Erechtheus, and Poseidon. If such an edifice in fact
existed, it was torn down to make way for a huge limestone platform, roughly 252 by 103 feet in size, that
was built as a base for the new temple. The slope of the
Acropolis was such that while on the north side the
foundations rested directly on bedrock, the southeast
corner needed to be built up with no less than twenty-
two courses, in order to correct a vertical drop of
thirty-five feet.

The actual base of the new temple was smaller than
the platform, as can still be clearly seen. The temple
itself was Doric, with a peristyle of six columns at each
end and sixteen along the sides. Except for the lowest
course in the base, the structure was to be built entirely
of Pentelic marble. This building project never reached
completion, for when the columns were still only half
erected and no more than a few courses of the inner
chambers, or cella, had been laid, all building on the
Acropolis abruptly ceased. Modern visitors to the
Acropolis can still see dark pinkish marks, indelibly
seared into the stone, that indicate where the Older
Parthenon's scaffolding went up in flames.

Ironically enough, while Athenian architects were
still laboring over their tribute to the victors of Marathon, a new crisis arose, one more serious than any
Athens had hitherto faced. Revenge for the burning of
Sardis and the defeat at Marathon had been postponed
for almost a decade by two fortunate accidents. The

autumn of 486 had brought a major rebellion in Egypt,
where Persian fiscal policies had caused widespread
unrest. Then, in November of that same year, Darius
died. For two years his son and chosen heir, Xerxes, had
been preoccupied with bringing Egypt to heel, a task
that he performed with systematic and highly effective
brutality. No sooner had Egypt been subjugated than
ambitious nobles at court, reinforced by equally ambitious Greek quislings anxious to seize or regain power
under Persian patronage, persuaded Xerxes to invade
Greece. By 484, disturbing reports of military preparations on a vast scale were reaching Athens. In every
shipyard of the Persian empire galleys and transports
were being built; a ship canal had been cut through
the Athos peninsula, and vast stockpiles of supplies
had begun to appear at strategic points along the coast
of Thrace. The object of all this activity was only too
clear to the alarmed Athenians.

Themistocles, who was as farsighted as he was practical, had anticipated such an attack from the very
beginning — unlike most of his countrymen, who seem
to have thought that the victory at Marathon meant
the end of the Persian threat. Indeed, all Themistocles's
political activities during the 480's were aimed at
strengthening Athens's ability to resist the storm when
it came. Potential Persian collaborators were ostracized,
and continuity in government — essential if Athens was
to weather a major crisis — was assured by the creation
of a board of generals, who, unlike the archons, could
be reelected annually. In the Assembly, Themistocles
reiterated the need for a strong fleet — only to be ob-
structed at every turn by conservative militarists who
were convinced that the propertied hoplites, the "men

of Marathon," were the solution to all Athens's ills. They looked down their superior noses at what they termed the "sailor rabble" who manned the rowing benches of the fleet. Thus in the face of danger Athens found herself dangerously divided. Quite apart from the social conflict involved, the average Athenian had only the vaguest notion of what the barbarians were really like, and he preferred to ignore the crisis until it blew up in his face.

Nothing better illustrates this widespread naïveté than the great debate occasioned when a rich new lode was struck in the Laurium silver mines. Deficient in exports and faced with the prospect of a cripplingly expensive war, the whole city should have seen what Aeschylus afterward called "this subterranean fount of silver" as a providential miracle. Instead, opposition to Themistocles, who wanted the state's profits earmarked for a new fleet, was so violent that it resulted in political deadlock. Themistocles's opponents proposed to share those profits with every Athenian citizen — at ten drachmas a head. Incredible as it may sound, the proposal was argued by no less a statesman than Aristides the Just. In the final showdown between Aristides and Themistocles, it was the former who lost and went into exile, but Themistocles's triumph did not wholly solve Athens's problems. There was barely time to build the fleet upon which the fate of Athens, Greece, and — arguably — all of Europe hung.

In the spring of 481 Xerxes' vast and heterogeneous host set out from Asia Minor: the invasion of Greece was finally under way. At this stage the chances of a Greek victory must have seemed minimal. Few of the major powers in central and northern Greece could be counted on to hold out against Xerxes, and some were already actively collaborating with him. Athens and Sparta, on the other hand, could not have done so even if they had wanted to. The Persian expedition was, after all, directed against them, and they had to either fight or go under. The Delphic Oracle, judging events with a cynically realistic eye, advised lesser states to maintain strict neutrality; for Athens she predicted sheer black disaster, with no escape save a flight to the world's end. By the spring of 480, with Xerxes already across the Hellespont and in northern Greece, it was plain that Athens, Sparta, and a handful of other states meant to fight. Themistocles wanted to undertake an amphibious holding action at Thermopylae and Artemisium — from which, if need be, they could fall back on Salamis and the isthmus.

Once again, however, Themistocles very nearly failed to get his way. Conservative forces were aligned against him, and their alternative strategy, that of holding central Greece at Tempe, was given up only when it became embarrassingly clear that the proposed position could be outflanked by at least two routes. The trouble was that Themistocles's plan, which was to man every available trireme and meet the invader as far forward in Greece as possible, would leave Athens itself without defenders, thus necessitating the city's total evacuation. The conservatives naturally regarded this prospect with horror. The very thought of abandoning their ancestral tombs and temples to barbarian ravishment was unthinkable. A second and even more cautious pronouncement from Delphi hardly improved matters, although it did offer Athens a scintilla of hope. "The wooden wall only shall not fail," the priestess asserted,

As Xerxes' troops closed in on Athens, the final
evacuation of the city took place—a plan of retreat
worked out months in advance by Themistocles and
later recorded on the remarkable tablet below,
which was discovered in 1959. Women, children,
and aged were to be evacuated to Troezen and
Salamis; all other Athenians were to "embark on
the 200 ships that lie ready and resist the barbarian
for the sake of their own freedom and that of the
rest of the Greeks." Such a vessel is shown on the
bas-relief from an ancient sarcophagus at left.

ending her prophecy with an ambiguous allusion to
Salamis. Themistocles naturally identified the wooden
wall as the new fleet; his opponents, anxious to defend
their holy places, argued that it was the timber palisade
topping the old wall on the Acropolis.

While Xerxes' forces advanced unopposed through
northern Greece, the argument raged. The Assembly
finally ratified Themistocles's proposals, but not before
decreeing that although the city itself was to be evacuated, some sort of defense force, together with the
priests of the various shrines, would be left behind to
hold the Acropolis against all comers. If one wooden
wall did not hold, the other might.

In the beginning it looked as if Themistocles's critics
would be vindicated, for despite some early naval successes off Artemisium and the immortal stand that King
Leonidas and his Spartans made at the Pass of Thermopylae, local intelligence work enabled Xerxes to
force the pass in a matter of days. Once Thermopylae
was lost, moreover, Artemisium became untenable as a
naval station. Themistocles pulled out his badly
mauled squadrons at once, sailed back home, organized
the final evacuation of Athens, and established an ad
hoc defense headquarters on the island of Salamis.
Athens's Peloponnesian allies, Sparta included, were
reported to be fortifying the isthmus and letting all
else go. Amid scenes of frantic chaos, every remaining
boat was pressed into service to ferry the city's civilian
evacuees to safety.

Meanwhile, on the Acropolis, Athens's last defenders
watched and waited. They dragged boulders and column drums into positions where they could be rolled
down on the attackers, and they did what they could —

Stripped of its sacred totems and abandoned by the government in 480, the Acropolis (opposite) stood naked before an advancing Persian army. A small residual force, encamped upon the citadel itself, was pledged to a final, foredoomed defense of the sacred precincts—but few had any hope that Athens could withstand the second major Persian invasion in less than a year. From the nearby island of Salamis, Themistocles and his government-in-exile watched the sea fill with Persian warships, even as Xerxes' troops began to move south from Mount Pentelicus. The victory at Marathon had proved hollow indeed, for ten years later the very fabric of Athenian life was threatened with obliteration.

using planks and old doors — to heighten the existing defenses. Their sense of abandonment was peculiarly acute, for Athena's precious image, the olive-wood totem, had been evacuated to Salamis with the government. In a sense, the residual force was defending an empty shell; even the goddess's sacred snake had mysteriously vanished. Rumor had it that Themistocles stage-managed both these events to persuade the superstitious that his evacuation scheme coincided with Athena's own wishes, but for those who stayed behind it was not an encouraging omen. From the great southwest bastion, the lookouts could see the Salamis channel aswarm with Greek triremes and transports. The road to the north, which wound its way between Hymettus and Pentelicus, was a source of even greater concern. Only a day later, Xerxes' first outriders came galloping down this road and into the deserted lower city.

Across Attica, the smoke from burning villages rose sluggishly into the blue summer air, marking the Persian army's line of advance. At this same time, the Persian fleet rounded Cape Sunium and was moving up the Saronic Gulf toward Phaleron, leaving a similar trail of destruction as it advanced. Strategically speaking, with all Attica lost this obstinate defense of the Acropolis made no sense. On the other hand, the moral and psychological lift provided by such a gesture — especially to the ships' crews at Salamis — was incalculable, and the Persians themselves knew this as well as anyone. After a desultory and largely symbolic devastation of the lower town, they therefore turned their attention to Athena's rock. The Greeks were well entrenched and stubbornly ingenious; flushing them out proved a surprisingly difficult task.

Xerxes' officers saw at once that their only chance lay in penetrating the defenses above the western slope, where the approach was less precipitous and the barricades might, with effort, be breached. They also perceived the essential weakness of the garrison's wooden wall: archers were stationed nearby on the Areopagus, from whence they shot fire arrows into the palisade protecting the Old Propylon. The timbers, bone dry from exposure to the blazing Mediterranean sun, at once crackled into flame — and Xerxes thereupon sent a group of Pisistratid collaborators to urge the garrison's surrender. This tactless offer met with a curt refusal; the Athenians, however desperate, had no intention of dealing with their treacherous countrymen.

A direct assault up the western ramp followed, but it was routed when the defenders rolled boulders and column drums down on their attackers. For a while, Xerxes was in something of a quandary. Then, on the advice of a local informant, he discovered the existence of the old stairway on the north face that led up to the sanctuary of Aglauros. This ascent involved a harrowing climb, but a group of bold Iranian mountaineers successfully negotiated it. As they emerged on the summit of the rock, at a point where no sentinels had been posted, the defenders panicked. Instead of containing the attack before it could proceed, they immediately assumed that all was lost. Some committed suicide by throwing themselves down from the walls; others sought sanctuary — just as Cylon's followers had done — in the Old Temple of Athena.

For the moment, the unopposed Persian commando force made no move against the Greek suppliants. Instead, with cool practicality, Xerxes' men threw open

the gates of the Old Propylon and let in the entire besieging force. Only then were the terrified defenders, priests included, dragged from sanctuary and put to the sword. This done, the Persians systematically stripped the shrines and temples of their valuables, smashed or pulled down what they could, and then set the buildings afire. The Greeks on Salamis were so shattered by the spectacle of smoke and flames rising from the Acropolis — knowing full well what this must mean — that many of them hastened aboard their triremes, ready for instant flight. To them, the fall of Athens's traditional stronghold and religious center was a profound catastrophe. Xerxes, too, seems to have regarded it as of symbolic importance, for he promptly sent a messenger to Susa, the Persian capital, to announce his total mastery over Athens. The next day, perhaps feeling that his actions had been overharsh if not actually sacrilegious, the Persian monarch sent for the Pisistratid exiles. At his behest, they climbed up to the fire blackened, still smoking summit of the Acropolis, where they made placatory sacrifices in the Greek manner. Upon their return they informed Xerxes that the black and calcined stump of Athena's sacred olive had miraculously put forth a fresh, eighteen-inch shoot overnight.

As a symbol of regeneration from disaster this omen proved remarkably apt, for within a month Themistocles had tempted the Great King's fleet into the narrows off Salamis and there dealt it a crushing defeat. From that moment the whole pattern of the war changed. Xerxes recalled what remained of his naval forces and returned home, leaving his son-in-law Mardonius and a streamlined professional army to police

Less than a month after Xerxes' soldiers put the
Acropolis to the torch and its defenders to the
sword, Themistocles's navy lured the Persian fleet
into the Salamis Channel and dealt it a mortal
blow. The war was far from over, but the Persian
offensive had been permanently blunted. Xerxes
recalled his main force to Asia Minor, and Greek
foot soldiers such as the one depicted on the grave
stele at left gradually reoccupied the mainland
By this time the ascendancy of Athena the
warrior-maiden made it altogether natural that
representations of the goddess should depict her in
full armor. The fragmentary remains of the
renowned Strangford shield (below) are thought to
duplicate the design of the shield affixed to the
image of Athena that once stood in the Parthenon.

Vowing not to rebuild any of the temples that had been burned in the course of the second Persian invasion, the Greeks turned to the more serious task of rebuilding their war-racked economy. For some thirty years the soot-stained temples on the Acropolis stood as blackened reminders of the Persian outrage. Then, gradually, the Greeks began rebuilding—with the same exuberance and on an even grander scale. The pedimental ornament below reveals a distinctive aspect of Greek architecture, the predilection for painting architectural details to accentuate their decorative qualities.

Attica and central Greece. In 479 Mardonius reoccupied Athens, and this time — presumably by way of revenge for the defeat at Salamis — the Persians razed the city completely. Only a few houses were spared, and these were used as billets for the Persian high command. On the Acropolis, Athena's half-built temple was torn down, leaving blocks and column drums scattered about the site. Shortly thereafter, a Peloponnesian army marched north from the isthmus and fought Mardonius at Plataea in Boeotia. His defeat freed Greece from the presence of a Persian army — and, as things turned out, from the threat of another invasion. It was not a peace, but at least it proved a durable armistice.

When the Athenians reoccupied their city they found it little more than a wasteland of cinders and rubble. Their mood at the time was a curious mixture of pride and practicality, patriotic flamboyance and civic foresight. Before the battle of Plataea each man had taken an oath that included the clause, "I will not rebuild any of the temples that have been burned and destroyed by the barbarians, but I will let them be left as a memorial, to those who come after, of the sacrilege of the barbarians." For thirty years this oath remained binding, and archaeological evidence indicates that with two minor exceptions the shrines on the Acropolis as well as those around the Agora were deliberately left in ruins until the mid-fifth century. Only after peace was formally concluded with Persia in 449 did the citizens of Athens feel morally absolved from their oath. It is no coincidence that the next few decades witnessed the most extraordinary efflorescence of temple architecture in Athenian history.

The two instances that might seem infringements of the Plataean Oath both involved archaic and sacred images, and it may well be that exceptions were made for their safekeeping. Athena's olive-wood totem had to take up residence on the Acropolis once more, and there was a debate over where it should be housed. Certainly not in the ruined Old Temple, which the Athenians were forbidden to rebuild. The solution seems to have been to construct a small temporary shrine, perhaps no more than a baldachin, in a precinct near the north face of the rock. A similar arrangement was made for the ancient statue of Athena Nike, who was reportedly represented as wingless so that she might never fly away and desert the Athenians when they had most need of her.

With these two minor exceptions, all new construction in Athens immediately after the war was secular and municipal. Here, in sharp contrast, we find evidence of widespread activity. Fortifications had to be restored against possible attack and the administration needed new government offices. Thus, the Persian sack offered a splendid opportunity for replanning the city on a grand scale. Demolition gangs and builders got to work at once. Top priority was given to the city walls, and at Themistocles's urging every able-bodied man, woman, and child was pressed into service for this task — "sparing neither private nor public edifice that would in any way help to further the work, but demolishing them all," according to Thucydides. Loose rubble, broken blocks — even marble reliefs and funeral steles — were thrown pell-mell into the fill. The Acropolis wall was also rebuilt, although that project remained uncompleted for some time and there are no signs of the frantic haste that marks the restoration of the perimeter wall. Modern visitors, walking below the north face of the Acropolis, are immediately struck by a series of column drums that have been carefully and symmetrically built into the upper bastion. These drums came from the ruined Older Parthenon — a perpetual reminder to Athenians of Persian vandalism.

During this period there was some secular construction work done on the Acropolis itself, since the rock was not only the home of Athena, but also the repository for state funds. Treasuries, or temple strong rooms, had to be built without delay — not that in those early postwar years Athens had any reserves to speak of. Indeed, for roughly a decade she seems to have tottered on the verge of insolvency — hence the persistent reuse of abandoned materials. A marked swing toward pro-Spartan conservatism eased Themistocles out of political office and forced him into exile in 471 on a trumped-up charge of collaboration with the Persians. His successor, a public hero, was Miltiades's wealthy and handsome son, Cimon — a competent soldier, a political dunderhead, and the darling of the reactionaries. Behind Cimon's various Aegean campaigns, plunder loomed large as an unacknowledged objective, although personal self-glorification was not forgotten either. Raiding Scyros, he not only cleared the island of pirates but brought home what were purported to be the bones of Theseus, Athens's hero. This neat piece of civic propaganda was welcomed with tumultuous enthusiasm — and not forgotten by astute politicians. Cimon's greatest success, on every count, was his smashing victory over Darius's land and sea forces in the battle of the Eurymedon in 466. In one stroke this victory crippled Persia's renascent naval power, opened the eastern Mediterranean to Greek shipping, and provided Athens — largely through Cimon's personal generosity — with a fantastic financial windfall in the form of captured booty.

It was after Eurymedon that Athens's building program, which had been more or less quiescent for a decade, got under way once more. The first edifice to rise was a splendid new council chamber with a circular base and a conical roof. It was followed by the famous Painted Stoa, or Colonnade, a long, cloisterlike structure on the north side of the Agora. This building housed shops and an art gallery where Athens's finest painters exhibited their work, and it was also a favorite gathering place for philosophers. Built with a pleasant view of the Acropolis, the Stoa soon became one of Athens's most familiar and characteristic landmarks.

Tradition ascribes the endowment of the Stoa to Cimon's brother-in-law, although Cimon himself was among the last of Athens's great private patrons of the classical period. It was he who cleared away ruined areas to create pleasant public squares, planted plane trees around the Agora, and completely redesigned the Academy, creating a green oasis of streams and shady avenues. It is not surprising that Cimon was, for a time, a highly popular figure in Athens, for he worked at his public image with relentless assiduity. His house always stood open to the public, and the orchards on his country estate could be stripped of their fruit by any passerby. If he failed to anticipate Pericles's program of architectural development on the Acropolis, that was only because the terms of the Plataean Oath specifically ruled out such a project. He did the next best thing,

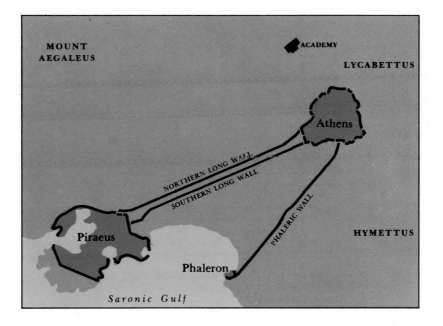

however. Forbidden to rebuild or restore the ambitious new temple undertaken to commemorate the victory at Marathon, he contented himself with extending the terrace underpinning the temple's massive foundations on the south side of the Acropolis. A great holding wall — now hidden by its medieval successor — was raised from the bastion, and into the space thus created went endless fragments of fire-scorched debris from the catastrophe of 480. The stage, in physical and architectural terms, was now set for the creation of the glorious Parthenon of Pericles.

Cimon's political exile in 459 marked a turning point in Athenian politics. For several years the conservative-aristocratic faction had been losing ground to a more radical and intellectual group, one that included the young Pericles among its members. Fierce attacks upon the entrenched privileges of the Areopagus Council succeeded in stripping its members of their powers and heralded a new stage in civic self-awareness. From that point on, private patronage was eradicated from public works, and much paternalism went with it. Henceforth it was the Assembly that decided what should or should not be built — on a public vote, with public construction records, and out of public funds. In this mood of growing confidence, the Athenian government — perhaps worried by a booming population and an increasing shortage of key commodities such as grain and timber — embarked upon an aggressively expansionist foreign policy. Her allies found themselves reduced to the status of imperial subjects rather than free members of an anti-Persian defensive league under Athens's leadership. Her neighbors, such as Boeotia, learned to fear her acquisitive grasp.

However, a string of military disasters in Egypt and elsewhere proved a sharp setback to Athenian ambitions abroad. In 454 the defensive league's treasury, hitherto on Delos, was transferred to Athens — ostensibly for safety, although less charitable explanations gained credibility when Athens began to systematically use league funds for her own benefit. In 451, Pericles and his colleagues were forced to conclude a five-year truce with Sparta. Indeed, in many ways the ratification of peace with Persia two years later was a desperation measure designed to win time against the hostile Peloponnesian states. For the history of the Parthenon, however, it proved nothing less than momentous, a crucial watershed in the development of Athens as an organic cultural monument that still evokes our awed admiration today.

IV

THE AGE OF PERICLES

In the spring of 449 B.C., immediately after the conclusion of peace with Persia, Pericles — who was by then the unquestioned leader of the democratic faction that had ruled Athens for over a decade — brought a somewhat unusual proposal before the Assembly. He proposed that all Greek cities, on the mainland and in Asia Minor, should be invited to send representatives to a panhellenic congress in Athens. "The subjects to be discussed," says Plutarch, "were the Greek sanctuaries which had been burned down by the Persians; the sacrifices owed to the gods on behalf of Hellas to fulfill the vows made when they were fighting the Persians; and the security of the seas, so that all ships could sail them without fear and keep the peace." Behind this seemingly harmless agenda much ingenious statecraft and civic ambition lay concealed. Any decision to restore Greece's burned sanctuaries would mean revoking the Plataean Oath, a step for which justification would have to be sought. As subsequent events made clear, the "sacrifices owed to the gods" would likewise be discharged, in part at least, by erecting new temples to commemorate the final victory over the Persians. Most important of all, however, was the last item on the agenda, the policing of the Aegean, since this could only be done effectively by the powerful and experienced Athenian fleet.

Pericles's objective was twofold: he hoped to win official, if tacit, endorsement for Athens's position as de facto leader of the Greek world, a claim that Sparta, for one, was unlikely to endorse; and at the same time, he planned to make a case for spending the defense league's money on a number of exclusively Athenian building projects. If Athens's rivals boycotted the congress, so much the better; she could then take unilateral action without consulting them further. In one sense, of course, to solicit such a conference at all was a confession of weakness. What a government cannot enforce, it must pursue through diplomacy — in spite of her dazzling reputation, Athens was in a decidedly shaky position. The democratic faction's recent attempts at territorial expansion had turned out badly, and the five-year truce with Sparta and the Peloponnesian bloc, concluded in 451, had only another three years to run. Moreover, Attica had recently suffered one grain famine and was soon to be hit by another. Perhaps worst of all, Pericles's accommodation with Persia had called into question all Athenian claims to be leading an anti-Persian defense league and had exposed her for what she was, an imperialist power dunning tribute from resentful subject-allies.

It would thus be a great mistake to assume that when he formulated his plan for a panhellenic congress Pericles was negotiating from strength. Among other things, Athens's financial future looked extremely perilous despite the Laurium mines. Unemployment loomed, a grim and politically inflammable threat to civil harmony. And with Persia and Athens no longer at war, the collection of tribute was hard to justify. Indeed, tribute seems to have been remitted throughout the empire in 448 — and despite this precaution there were ominous rumblings of revolt.

So ruinous an indulgence could not be granted indefinitely, of course; imperial tribute must continue to fill Athens's coffers at any cost and in any guise. Pericles's notion was simply to redesignate those funds for the maintenance of security on the high seas. As for

the leadership of Greece, if Athens could not arrogate this by force, then she must justify her claims in other, less tangible ways. Cultural, religious, and intellectual supremacy was henceforth to be her watchword; Athenian greatness would be sold, visibly and irrefutably, with splendid moral uplift and civic panache, to the entire Greek world. This was not in itself a new program, of course, and unkind opposition wags lost no time in labeling Pericles and his friends "Pisistratids." It was the sheer scale and quality of their achievement that set them in a class by themselves.

The nickname was understandable, for Pericles no less than Pisistratus knew the value of civic and religious propaganda — as his subsequent actions make very plain. True, the iron fist of imperialism was busily establishing a strategic network of colonial outposts and building up the Athenian fleet, but it did wear the velvet glove of culture. In archaeologist T. Leslie Shear's apt phrase, "If Athens was to become the center of the civilized world, she must again play hostess to the Muses." Power and glamour were to go hand in hand. The Panathenaic festival, it was hoped, would attract visitors from every corner of the Greek world. Mystical initiation was offered at the Eleusinia, while the Greater Dionysia provided dramatic entertainment — not to mention an ostentatious, onstage display of allied tribute. But how, Pericles must have asked, could such ceremonies be performed without a stage truly worthy of them? The Acropolis, natural symbol of Athenian greatness, was still largely a ruined monument to Persian vandalism. It was clearly time to abrogate the Plataean Oath and, using accumulated league tribute, fund a building program such as Greece had

never seen. To this end Pericles conceived the gambit of a panhellenic congress.

There were also certain financial considerations underlying the Athenian leader's move. By the time the league treasury was shifted from Delos to Athens in 454, it had an accumulated reserve of 30,000,000 drachmas, equal in value to almost eleven tons of pure gold. And while this sum was a godsend for Pericles's immediate purposes, it would neither support the fleet indefinitely nor pay for the restoration of every sacked temple. Thus, on more than one count, the reestablishment of tribute was essential — as Pericles could, and did, argue — for maintaining law and order on the high seas while at the same time discharging those religious debts incurred at the time of the Persian wars. Predictably, when it came to a showdown the Peloponnesian bloc, headed by Sparta, boycotted the congress. Other states followed suit, and as a result the proposed meeting was not held at all.

Since Athens's own subject-allies voiced no opinion in the matter, Pericles now felt free to pursue his building scheme as a purely domestic issue. He ran into a maelstrom of domestic controversy almost at once, however, a controversy that polarized conservative and progressive opinion in Athens as never before. Since Cimon's death in 450, the conservative-aristocratic faction had been led by Thucydides (not the historian but the son of Melesias). These aristocrats regarded Pericles's grandiose project with intense suspicion; to traditionalists everywhere it seemed arrogant, morally dubious, and a wanton waste of public funds. Unable to block Pericles's project, they subjected it to severe harassment— at least until 445, when Thucydides was

By the spring of 449 the decades-old war with Persia
was drawing to a close, and battlefield combat—the
subject of the contemporary vase painting shown
below—had given way to serious negotiation of
treaty terms. As soon as an armistice had been signed,
a young democrat named Pericles, whose bust is
seen opposite, began the most impressive program of
public works in Greek history. Among his creations
were the Propylaea, the first Odeon, and the very
symbol of Periclean Athens, the Parthenon itself.

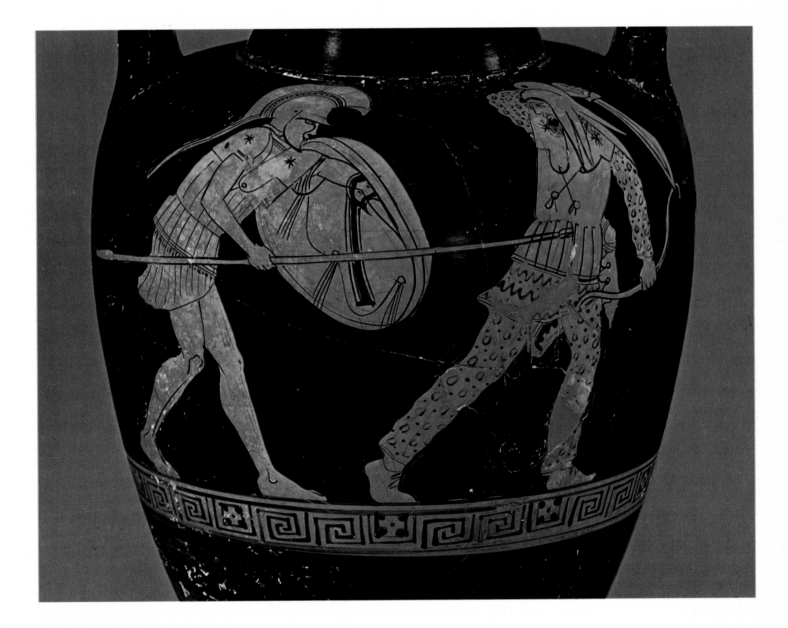

sent into political exile, and Pericles embarked upon fifteen successive years of unbroken power. Extravagance was the main charge leveled against Pericles, and it was repeated again and again. "The Greeks must be outraged," Thucydides thundered. "They must consider this an act of bare-faced tyranny, when they see that with their own contributions, extorted from them by force for the war against the Persians, we are gilding and bedizening our city, which, for all the world like a wanton woman, adds to her wardrobe precious stones and costly statues and thousand-talent temples." This last gibe, at least, was a wild exaggeration; the Parthenon probably cost less than half that sum. But there was enough plausibility in the charges to create a sizable and persistent opposition caucus.

There also seemed to be a good deal more civic self-aggrandizement than religious devotion in the planners' motivating principles. Pericles himself had a reputation for freethinking rationalism, and it was no accident that "impiety" was a favorite charge brought against him and his associates. It is clear that he regarded the state cults as one more instrument for attaining his cultural and political ends — and here his critics broke company with him, for commemorating victory and honoring the gods were, in their opinion, objectives that called for moderation. Indeed, the proposal, made early in 449, to rebuild the little Shrine of Athena Nike and provide it with a permanent priestess may well have come from the conservative faction — but it was Pericles and his supporters who got this project overruled in favor of their own larger vision. Quite apart from this affront to their sense of piety and moderation, the conservatives were worried by Peri-

cles's much-publicized promise that his building scheme would offer widespread employment to artisans of every sort. Reactionaries viewed the concept of government subsidies to such rabble as nothing less than radical nonsense.

Yet Pericles got his way, both concerning the Acropolis building program and the expansion of the fleet. The Assembly ratified proposals to lay down ten new triremes annually, to reallocate the 30,000,000 drachmas for construction work on the Acropolis, and to fund this account with an additional 18,000,000 drachmas when the scheme was well advanced. From this point on the conservatives could not stop Pericles in principle, only call for some curb upon his grandiose design. Even here they had little success, for why should any member of the Athenian Assembly vote himself out of a good job? Carpenters, stonemasons, dyers, painters, engravers, wagonmakers, stonecutters and quarrymen, teamsters, muleteers, ropemakers, roadbuilders, clerks, miners, and unskilled laborers ad infinitum — all had the franchise and all hoped to share in some profitable, long-term contract.

Pericles's plans were no secret; they had been discussed at endless meetings of both the Council and the Assembly, and pored over by innumerable subcommittees. They included the great Temple of Athena that was later known as the Parthenon; a lavish reconstruction of the Propylaea; a new style musical auditorium, the Odeum, that was to be erected beside the Theater of Dionysus; a sumptuous Hall of the Mysteries at Eleusis; and perhaps the Temple of Hephaestus — popularly but erroneously known as the Theseum — that still survives, almost intact, on the west side of the

Agora. Whatever happened, there would be no shortage of work. And those unemployed citizens who were too idle, ignorant, or troublesome to find a place in the great project could always be shipped off to one of the new colonial settlements, outposts of empire that also proved a useful dumping ground for subversives and misfits of every stripe.

Meanwhile, as a prime objective, the temple on the south side of the Acropolis — the structure raised in 488 to honor Athens's victory at Marathon and burned down by the invading Persians eight years later while still half-built — was to be reconstructed in the most impressive manner that human genius could devise. It would be a monument to Athena the warrior-maiden, patroness of learning — and through Athena it would honor the supreme deity, her father, Zeus. Its soaring splendor and architectural subtleties would testify with eloquence to Athenian wealth, intellect, and artistic imagination. To avoid any taint of hubris, even those patriotic achievements exemplified in the temple's decorative sculptures would emphasize Athenian avoidance of excess and respect for moral law. The conflict of the Centaurs and the Lapiths, or Theseus's famous battle against the Amazons — did not such themes suggest the triumph of civilization and restraint over unbridled barbarism? And would not those who saw them be reminded, simultaneously, of Athens's glorious stand against less mythical forces of darkness during the Persian wars?

This central theme was to be repeated in the gigantic gold and ivory statue of Athena that was to provide the new temple with its inner focal point. Amazons appeared on the outside of Athena's shield, giants on

the inside, Centaurs and Lapiths on the goddess's sandals — and these motifs, here as on the temple's pediments and metopes, were calculated to remind a visitor of what Athena, and a fortiori Athens, stood for in moral terms — civilization, order, self-restraint, and creativity. Like the frescoes adorning a Byzantine basilica, the sculptures of the Parthenon were to provide visual propaganda, in the broadest sense of the term.

To realize this ambitious program, to clothe Pericles's political and cultural message in the habiliments of true art, called for a genius of rare vision — and the moment brought forth such a man. In truth, Phidias, son of Charmides, was already a famous sculptor by 449. Some years previously he had executed the gigantic bronze statue of Athena whose spear and helmet could be seen glinting in the sunlight by sailors rounding Cape Sunium. Pericles commissioned Phidias not only to create the goddess's new cult statue — in itself a monumental task — but also to exercise general supervision over the whole Acropolis program. It was, as things turned out, an inspired choice. Working with Phidias were the architects Callicrates and Ictinus, about whom little is known. Ictinus, to judge from his name, was probably not an Athenian. In any event he came to Athens from the western Peloponnese, where he had executed another impressive Doric temple, the Arcadian shrine of Apollo at Bassae. Callicrates had drawn up the plans for the Temple of Athena Nike, the design that had been shelved in favor of Pericles's more ambitious project. When working out their designs and estimates for official approval, these men were constantly reminded of the political controversy raging over their heads in the Assembly. As has been noted,

the main charge leveled at Pericles by his opponents was that of willful extravagance. He countered this accusation by instructing the architects to reuse the blocks and column drums of the Older Parthenon — which thus in a very material sense came to influence its more famous successor. The steps of the cella and stylobate of the new temple were identical in height to those of the old, and — more important for the temple's fundamental proportions — the lower diameter of both porch and peristyle columns also corresponded. In addition, Cimon's engineers had done such a good job on the new southern wall that both base and foundations could still be used — one key reason for the remarkable speed with which the Parthenon arose when building actually began.

It is significant that the Periclean center of emphasis on the Acropolis lay well away from the hallowed complex of shrines by the north face, for that reorientation underscores the fact that the Parthenon was designed, first and foremost, as a monument to human achievement. This fact was subsequently driven home by the Propylaea, the most lavish example of purely secular architecture that Athens had ever seen. The "children of Erechtheus," as Euripides somewhat grandiloquently termed his fellow countrymen, might enjoy Zeus' bounty through the intercession of Athena, but they did not underrate their own contributory efforts either. To the gods all due honor — yet was not man the measure of all things? Great victories in the Persian wars, the subsequent burgeoning of intellectual and artistic creativity, the spread of imperial dominion — these triumphs were undoubtedly fresh in the minds of Pericles's builders when they began working out

themes for the new temple's unparalleled profusion of sculptural adornment.

The aforementioned Ionic frieze of the cella, no less than 524 feet long and portraying the various stages of the Panathenaic procession, was a stylish adaptation of myth to civic pride, a leitmotiv that recurs in one guise or another throughout the sculptures. We know that during this commission Phidias worked in close consultation with Pericles, and consequently there can be little doubt that the Parthenon sculptures were meant to express, in visual form, those basic aims and ideals to which the Athenian leader subscribed.

Like the frieze, both pediments and all ninety-two metopes were crowded with figures. The central theme of these panels — the triumph of rational civilization over savagery, violence, and the forces of darkness — emerges from the reliefs with unambiguous clarity. Drunken, lecherous Centaurs — hybrid monsters dear to the primitive psyche — are routed by law-abiding, responsible men through collective social action. The giants, those personifications of primeval chaos and bestial, arbitrary power, are vanquished by Zeus and his Olympian warriors.

This major theme is threaded, with subtle and unobtrusive skill, into a local heroic setting. Encapsulating the whole mise-en-scène are the two great pedimental compositions, which have, alas, been sadly mutilated. Fortunately, we possess Pausanias's eyewitness testimony concerning their subject matter. According to him, the western pediment portrayed Athena's struggle with Poseidon for the possession of Attica, while the eastern one showed her birth from Zeus' head. The western façade depicts Theseus and his

followers struggling with the Amazons. Plutarch tells us that their battle was supposedly fought just west of the Acropolis, between Museum Hill and the Pnyx — a topographical reference that gives an extra dimension to the ancient myth. Through cross-references to Attica's heroes and legends the timeless was made to intersect with time, and the mind was directed, by such specific association, to more human, historically identifiable achievements.

More suggestive still are the few surviving metopes on the north side, since these record dramatic highlights from the siege and capture of Troy. By 449, the use of Troy as a symbolic or mythical equivalent for Persia was already well established, and it would not be difficult for a patriotic Athenian, when surveying the Parthenon, to remember his immediate rather than his more remote ancestors. In secular buildings, where there was no need for an oblique approach, civic propagandists had a field day. The Odeum, for example, was not only roofed with spars and timbers from captured Persian galleys but designed as a replica of the Great King's pavilion as well.

Theseus victorious over the invading Amazons, Athena meeting and besting Poseidon — such themes carried suggestive and exhilarating overtones. But the ultimate message of the Parthenon sculptures was clearly that while Zeus and Athena preside over all, the concept of Athens triumphant, of man in his pride and his glory, permeates every aspect of Athenian life. Even in the great frieze, the civic procession is of more importance than the goddess whom it honors. Small wonder that pious conservatives viewed the whole project with such intense suspicion.

It took two years of detailed planning before all specifications were approved, every contract for labor and materials let, and work on the Parthenon could actually begin. The first stone was laid on July 28, 447, during the Panathenaic festival. Separate boards of overseers were appointed for the temple and its cult statue, the importance — and cost — of which should not be underestimated. To the casual observer it must have seemed that Pericles envisaged no more than an elaborate restoration of the Older Parthenon, on the same foundation base and with roughly identical dimensions. Such observations woefully underestimated Phidias and his associates, however, for although they reused blocks wherever possible they also built throughout in the pure white Pentelic marble, an unprecedented extravagance.

The same expansive attitude can be seen in their treatment of the Parthenon's overall proportions. The normal Doric temple had six columns in its façade and thirteen down each side. This ratio — of 6 : 6 × 2 + 1 — was disrupted in certain cases, the two Parthenons included, by the ritual need for an extra chamber beyond the cella, which made for a long, narrow floor plan. Here the architects of the Parthenon completely broke with tradition. Rather than merely increase the number of columns in the peristyle, they broadened the façade to eight columns — thus restoring the proportional ratio — and similarly extended the cella. To avoid any impression of squat lumpishness, the columns of the façade were made finer and taller than the Doric norm and set uncharacteristically close together.

Among other things, this innovation enabled Phidias to experiment with interior space when executing and

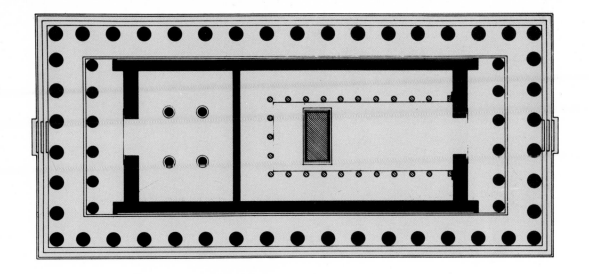

siting his colossal cult statue of Athena. Rather than place it tamely and conventionally against the back wall of the cella, he set its base well forward, isolating it further by means of an internal peristyle (see diagram above). The construction of this image, reputedly almost forty feet in height, base included, must in itself have been a formidable undertaking. A huge vertical beam, rising from a central floor socket, served as an armature. To support the statue's arms, Phidias may have employed an iron core inserted through the vertical beam at the point of balance. The statue itself was then built up by means of shaped and bonded wooden blocks held to the armature by internal struts. Over this surface, finally, was fitted a sheath of gold and ivory plates. The gold plates, reasonably enough, were made detachable for inspection, since they came from state funds and were worth a king's ransom. Ivory was used on the feet, hands, and face to represent the goddess's flesh — an appropriate choice, for it was both milk pale and costly. Athena's eyes glinted with gems; her left hand rested on her shield, and in her right she held aloft a crowned Victory. Above her helmet, between winged griffins, crouched an inscrutable sphinx. The overall effect, in that crepuscular half-light, must have been nothing short of overwhelming — if a trifle garish for modern taste.

The first year of construction was consumed almost entirely with quarrying and transporting marble from Mount Pentelicus — that pure white, finely grained stone that, because of its slight iron content, weathers to the pale honey gold so characteristic of the Parthenon itself. This part of the work, too often ignored or taken for granted, presented formidable obstacles that

were overcome only with extraordinary ingenuity. One can still see the chisel marks where rectangular blocks were first cut and then split away from the rest of the excavation by means of water-soaked — and consequently expanding — wooden wedges. More hazardous still was the business of transportation, especially during the first stages, when the quarried blocks had to be brought down a steep and rocky mountainside from heights of between two and three thousand feet. The blocks had to be maneuvered on sleds down a paved quarry road (parts of which still survive), and only the smaller ones could be eased along on rollers. At intervals there were stout posts, carrying rope and tackle, which were used to help brake the sleds' downward momentum. Accidents were not unknown, and one rough-dressed column drum, probably destined for the Parthenon, lies in a nearby ravine to this day.

Even when the plain was safely reached, difficulties still abounded. Shifting a total of 22,000 tons of marble across ten miles of level plain to the Acropolis proved a major operation in itself. These drums, blocks, and architraves were so enormously heavy that special methods of transport had to be devised for them, and the existing road had to be rebuilt so that it was strong enough to support their weight. Traffic was restricted to the dry summer months for fear that the blocks would bog down in the mud, and the largest blocks of all seem to have baffled the wagonmakers. Axles had to be inserted directly into their end sockets, and these were then equipped with wheels no less than twelve feet in diameter. The whole was fitted to a frame of four-inch timbers and drawn by up to thirty teams of oxen. Shifting a block of marble from the

The designers of the Parthenon expanded the classic dimensions of the Doric temple in all directions, and as a result Athena's new temple boasted a greater number of columns than any predecessor. Tapering and converging at the same time, they seemed to lift the entire building into the Attic sun (far right). At the center of the Parthenon's generous floor plan stood a huge new cult statue of Athena, almost forty feet high from base to crown. This Athena's ivory skin and gold raiment, bolted over a wooden core, cost the Athenian government nearly as much as the temple itself. Removed to Constantinople in A.D. 400, the statue subsequently disappeared. Thus Phidias's greatest work survives only in miniature, its essential details supposedly preserved in the second-century B.C. copy at near right.

quarry to the Acropolis took at least two days and cost up to 300 drachmas — at a time when one drachma was the average laborer's daily wage. Then, at the foot of the Acropolis itself there was more sweating with sleds and rollers, pulleys and tackle before the blocks could finally be maneuvered into position atop the citadel for the stonemasons to dress.

"So the buildings arose," says Plutarch, "as imposing in their sheer size as they were inimitable in the grace of their outlines, since the artists strove to excel themselves in the beauty of their workmanship." Highly skilled sculptors and masons worked diligently year after year for what were surely, even by contemporary standards, little more than day-laborers' wages. There is a story, perhaps apocryphal, that when one of the overtired wagon mules was turned loose for a rest, it came back to the works of its own accord, trotting alongside its yokemates and even leading the way for them, as though exhorting and inciting them on. The Assembly purportedly decreed that so enthusiastically patriotic a beast should be maintained at public expense for the rest of its life, like a victorious athlete.

Not all such displays of goodwill were as altruistic, however. As Pericles had foreseen, the project provided employment for all sorts of workers over a number of years, and there can have been few citizens who failed to draw some benefit from it, if only indirectly. Athenians became inured to the endless clink of hammer and chisel, to overseers shouting orders, and to the sight of long dusty teams of oxen plodding up the Panathenaic Way with their massive loads of freshly cut marble bright against the cobalt sky.

At first, work on the Parthenon seems to have moved

slowly. Indeed, the first three years were largely spent quarrying blocks and drums and laying out the courses of the stylobate. This last was a particularly tricky operation because Phidias and his associates planned a very slight convex curvature in the horizontal line of the temple's base, one that would affect all other horizontals throughout the structure. As a result, the shape of the stylobate had to be precisely right; a whole system of subtle optical illusion depended on it.

Paradoxically, nothing in formal architecture looks less straight than a straight line; vertically it wilts, horizontally it sags. In a temple the size of the Parthenon this created a very real problem. Armed with mathematical expertise and remarkable aesthetic flair, Phidias and his two fellow architects set out to defeat the shortcomings of the human eye. Not only the stylobate, but also the columns rising from it were given a gentle, swelling curve. More striking still, these columns were all made to lean fractionally inward toward the cella, thus creating an impression of soaring perspective. (It has been calculated that if extended upward those columns would converge at a point one and a half miles above the Acropolis.) Variations in the spacing of columns and metopes added depth and solidity to the façades, and other refinements enhanced the overall visual impression, creating a sense of dynamic tension.

The superstructure of the Parthenon was largely built during the years 444–441, and it is surely no accident that in 442 Sophocles staged his *Antigone,* perhaps the supreme expression of Athens's fundamental, perennial conflict between clan and *polis,* kinship and law, affection and reason. Both works of art were conceived against the same background, and both embody the quintessence of fifth-century Athens at her apogee. Work on the Parthenon's metopes and frieze continued throughout this building period. The great cult statue of Athena was likewise progressing, and only the sculptures on the pediments had to wait until the rest of the temple was complete. In 440 the great doors were set in place — and subsequently embellished with the most elaborate ornamentation. Paneled and studded in bronze with animal heads, ivory inlay, and gold rosettes adorning the panels themselves, these doors formed a worthy entrance to the shrine. Roof beams, coffered ceilings, and wooden grilles were also now set in place; the giant statue, complete at last, gleamed on its plinth; and at the Panathenaic festival of 438, less than ten years after their inception, temple and statue were formally dedicated to Athena.

We are so accustomed to the chaste and broken whiteness of those timeworn columns that it is hard for us to envisage the Parthenon as it looked upon its completion. Time has removed all trace of color from its stones, but perhaps that is just as well for modern taste, since the Greeks had a passion for gilding or painting any stone surface in sight, and the Parthenon received more gilt than most. Its sculptures were especially lavishly decorated, with colored glass added to highlight eyes, for example. The apex of each pediment sprouted huge, writhing stone tendrils and acanthus leaves, and moldings ran riot. The general impression was, first and foremost, of an almost baroque clutter, hubris sanctified by religion and justified through art. The second impression was inevitably of expense, for it was impossible to contemplate either temple or statue without counting the cost and perhaps reflecting

Phidias's grand design for the Acropolis called for the grandest of building material—white marble from the slopes of Mount Pentelicus, ten miles northeast of Athens. In the quarries of Pentelicus, great blocks of stone were rough-dressed by local workmen in preparation for the hazardous descent to the Athenian plain. At the base of the Acropolis, the dray teams that had transported the marble from the foot of Pentelicus were abandoned in favor of pulleys and heavy tackle, used to hoist the stones to the site. Over the centuries, those massive blocks (below) have assumed a distinctive honey color, the result of gradual oxidation of the iron particles in the marble itself.

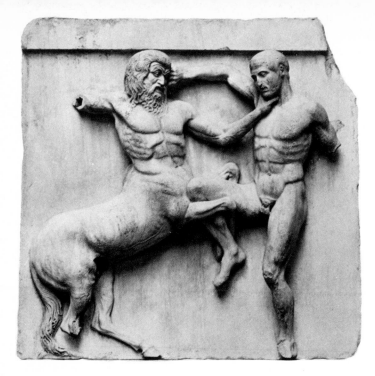

upon the tribute that had largely underwritten the creation of both. This Athena was simply imperial Athens writ large. It was not in her honor that the Panathenaic procession took place or the ancient image received its new, lovingly woven robe; the Parthenon was, ultimately, a monument not to Athena but to the Periclean ideal of cultured imperialism.

Understandably, no single item in the entire building program aroused as much hostile criticism as Phidias's statue. If the concept bespoke megalomania, the cost suggested pure spendthrift lunacy. Over 2,500 pounds of gold — worth more than 3,500,000 drachmas — had gone into it, and another 1,386,000 drachmas had been expended on ivory, wood, sculptors' fees, and miscellaneous expenses. By any estimate the total bill far outstripped the cost of the Parthenon itself. Small wonder then that despite the most stringent official precautions wild rumors of large-scale graft and embezzlement circulated during the statue's construction. Immediately after the dedication, charges were brought against Phidias, and vigorous efforts were made to involve Pericles himself in the scandal. Libelous fragments preserved from comedies of the day show that the political opposition, though crippled, had by no means given up. Phidias reportedly detached and weighed the gold plates to prove his innocence, but feelings were running so high that he judged it advisable to leave town in some haste rather than stand trial. He went to Olympia, where a commission for a giant statue of Zeus awaited him. His last workshop, complete with signed drinking mug and the molds he used to fashion metal drapery, has recently been discovered in Olympia, where, probably in 433, the sculp-

tor died without ever having returned to Athens.

As soon as work eased off on the Parthenon, most of the skilled labor force was transferred to the Propylaea. Pericles and his colleagues envisaged this latter edifice as a suitably magnificent entrance gate to the Acropolis in general and to their own new temple in particular. Surprise has sometimes been expressed that the program made no provision for restoring the archaic temple of Athena Polias, but civic splendor rather than traditional religious sentiment clearly had top priority. The Old Propylon was swept away and a new gateway was begun under the architectural supervision of Mnesicles. His plans were to some extent circumscribed by religious requirements, for the existence of the Athena Nike bastion and the precinct of Artemis Brauronia meant that the Propylaea had to be drastically foreshortened at its southern extremity. There were also various purely physical obstacles to overcome — not the least of which were changes in elevation that necessitated the construction of several hipped roofs if the façade were to present anything approaching an impression of structural unity.

Most important of all, Mnesicles's plan called for a radical new orientation. From Mycenaean times onward any western entrance gate had been laid out along a northeast-southwest axis. The new Mnesiclean ground plan was aligned more or less squarely on the four major compass points, so that a visitor to the Acropolis ascended the rock from due west, looking along a line parallel to the axis of the Parthenon. As he passed through the columned entrance porch he caught his first glimpse of Athena's great temple from the bottom of a gentle rise, where the architects' tricks

Above and left: three panels from the incomparable collection of Parthenon sculpture—known collectively as the Elgin Marbles—now in the British Museum. Overleaf: the Parthenon, picked to its marble bones by Lord Elgin and others, seems reduced to line and shadow.

of foreshortening and perspective further enhanced the impression of overwhelming grandeur. The two buildings had been planned in direct and harmonious relationship to one another; scale and proportion matched so exactly that in later ages men spoke of the two of them as the supreme achievement of Periclean architecture.

The outbreak of hostilities in 431 B.C. — the first phase of the Peloponnesian Wars — meant an abrupt cessation of building activities throughout Attica. Work on the Propylaea was suspended — for the duration, it was hoped; forever, as things turned out. By this time, however, the main project had been brought to completion. Mnesicles's design, though ambitious, was fundamentally simple: a central, templelike porch flanked on either side by two independent wings or annexes. (It was the annexes' inner chambers, both north and south, that were never finished.) The porch, with its Doric façade, contained one main gateway for wheeled traffic or draft animals and four passages for pedestrians. The coffered ceiling had a design of gold stars and palmettes on a blue ground. The annex known as the Pinakotheke seems to have been planned as a combined picture gallery and banqueting hall. The project was under construction for five years, and the total cost is given as 2,012 talents, or no less than 12,072,000 drachmas. As an overall estimate for the entire program — Parthenon, Propylaea, and statue of Athena — such a figure would be just barely plausible. Even so, it represents no more than one-fifteenth of the cost of the Peloponnesian War, and it incontestably produced more lasting and worthwhile results.

During the fateful years when the Acropolis building program was in full swing, many events of vital concern to Athens were taking place in other areas. In the field of letters we find Herodotus putting the final touches to his history of the Persian wars, while both Sophocles and Euripides were in midcareer as dramatists. Historically, this period between the wars was one of steadily mounting tension, and records reveal that Athens was forced to take ever-tougher measures to keep her subject-allies loyal and force punctual tribute out of them. Samos and Byzantium revolted under the increased pressure, and in 440 they had to be reduced by a full-scale punitive expedition. Pericles, delivering a funeral eulogy over the young Athenians who died during this campaign, said it was as though the spring had gone out of the year.

Relations with Sparta and the Peloponnesian League, which had been deteriorating steadily for some time, reached a new low when Pericles imposed economic sanctions against the little isthmus state of Megara in an unsuccessful effort to blackmail the Peloponnesian states. Protesting embassies reached Athens from Sparta, calling upon her to "give the Greeks back their freedom." Such appeals came far too late, however, for Athens was irrevocably committed to a policy of imperialist domination. This inevitably meant a final showdown with Sparta, and in 431 the war that Pericles had long seen coming — and against which he had stockpiled such vast reserves — was finally declared. With jingoistic self-confidence the Athenians embarked upon a conflict that only ran its final course some twenty-seven years later, by which time the Athenians had squandered all of the capital — tangible and intangible — that their brave experiment in democratic imperialism had built up.

V

THE STRUGGLE
FOR EMPIRE

The Peloponnesian War witnessed the final and brightest flare-up of Athenian creativity. What followed, although no less intellectually adventurous, was a new departure, an age of prose, scholarship, and philosophy, astronomy and mathematics, oratory and law. Focusing upon fourth-century Athens, with its growing emphasis on individualism and urban affluence, is like glimpsing our own world through the wrong end of a telescope, and that very similarity makes us realize all the more clearly what a gulf separates both worlds from the Periclean Age. Indeed, as a cultural totality that brilliant earlier flowering did not survive the fifth century. For some thirty-four years, from 438 to 404, the Parthenon did fulfill its original function, however, serving as a proud symbol of Athens's imperial triumph and intellectual achievement, the distilled essence of the *polis* ideal. From then on it slid imperceptibly into its role as a monument to vanished glories, a Proustian reminder of *temps perdu,* tangible proof — in days when proof was needed — that little Athens had once ruled the Aegean. The memorial became an imposing ruin, the ruin a sanctified tourist trap. The moment of perfection and truth had been all too brief.

What was true of the Acropolis monuments applied equally to those great literary landmarks of the fifth century, Attic tragedy and comedy. These, too, failed to outlive the special conditions that had brought them into being, and we search succeeding literary epochs in vain for a second Aeschylus or Aristophanes. As Athens's defeat in the Peloponnesian War drew near, there came, under the stimulus and stress of wartime conditions, one last tremendous upsurge of creative activity. The majority of Sophocles's and Euripides's surviving datable plays — including *Oedipus Rex, Maidens of Trachis, Electra,* and *Bacchae* — were written during the Peloponnesian War. All of Aristophanes's comedies also fall within a twenty-seven year span except for *The Women in Politics* and *Plutus* — and the latter is so remote in spirit from the author's early work that it not only seems to belong to a different world but might as well have been written by some altogether different playwright.

Thus the Peloponnesian War is not only a period of military and political history immortalized by Thucydides, it also forms a critical phase in Athens's final cultural development. This paradigm applies throughout, from Pericles's original committal to war in 431 to Lysander's entry into Athens, the pulling down of the Long Walls, and the installation of a Spartan garrison on the Acropolis in 404. For Athens, there were moments of triumph before the final tragedy, and it is significant that such occasions tend to be associated with some resumption of the Acropolis building program. Callicrates's long-postponed shrine to Athena Nike — replete with victory statue — was brought to completion in 425, about the same time that Sparta sued for peace after losing 120 Spartiate warriors on Sphacteria. The Altar of the Twelve Gods was also rebuilt, and work on the Erechtheum began soon after the conclusion of an armistice between Athens and Sparta. The link between civic or military glory and monumental building activities, especially on the Acropolis, was very close indeed.

The war as a whole falls naturally into three distinct sections. First was the Archidamian War, a tenyear period from the outbreak of hostilities to the signing of the Peace of Nicias in 421. It is named after the Spartan king Archidamus, who at intervals throughout the decade led a series of devastating raids into Attica. Next came what might be termed a phony peace, which lasted from 421 until the collapse of Athens's ill-fated expedition against Sicily in 413. Finally there was the Ionian War, during which hostilities were resumed between Athens and Sparta, largely in the eastern Aegean, and the former's last naval reserves were shattered. Each of these periods corresponded to a distinct phase in an Athenian social, cultural, and creative evolution that saw confidence give way to hysteria, class divisions harden, political groupings polarize into mutually hostile extremist juntas, and comedy become black farce.

During the early years of the Archidamian War, Pericles pursued what military strategists would describe as a fish-and-fox campaign. While Spartan hoplites ravaged Attica unopposed, Athenian naval units raided Megara and the Peloponnese. Sparta had no fleet worth the name as yet, and Pericles would not let Athenian troops meet the terrible Spartan phalanx in battle. This decision can be seen in retrospect as an appalling psychological blunder on Pericles's part, for his admission that Athenians were no match for Spartans on the battlefield hardly improved morale. Nor did the evacuation, and subsequent despoilment, of the Attica countryside. Refugees crowded into Athens, camping between the Long Walls and even invading the Pelargikon precinct below the Acropolis. The Spartans were thus free to destroy crops, burn farmhouses, and hack down vines and olive trees at leisure. The loss in economic terms was bad enough, but un-

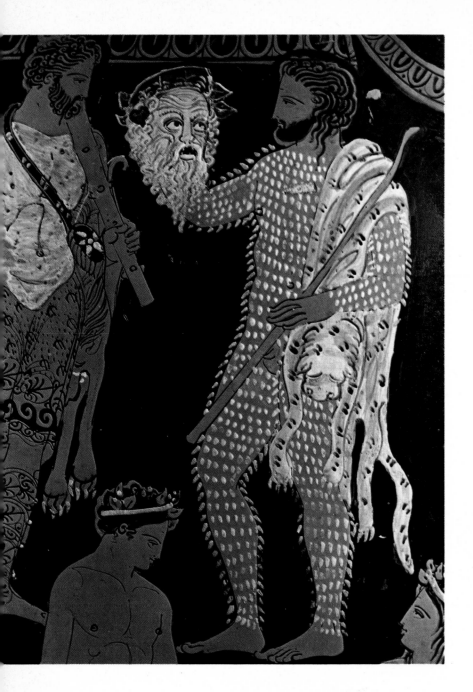

Athens's defeat in the Peloponnesian War brought her brief Golden Age to an inglorious close. The history of those bitter years was immortalized by Thucydides, antiquity's greatest historian; the spirit of the era was recorded in another fashion, by a handful of inspired playwrights. Aeschylus, Sophocles, Euripides, Aristophanes—all saw their works performed in outdoor theaters such as the Theater of Dionysus at right, below. Masks, an integral part of these productions, were a feature of contemporary art, as the bas-relief below indicates. It shows the fourth-century-B.C. playwright Menander examining the masks worn by the players in one of his comedies. These disguises ranged from the grotesque (left, below) to the strikingly naturalistic (left), and included a wide range of easily recognized emotions, as the handsome mosaic shown at right reveals.

Museums preserve the frozen marble features of fifth-century Athens's intellectual vanguard—which was led by the philosopher Socrates (right, above) and the dramatist Sophocles (right, below), among others—but neither statue matches the vigor or intensity of the bronze portrait head at left. The intellectual fervor that marked the closing decades of that century burns with enduring incandescence in those eyes, conveying the conceptual energy of the era to the most casual passer-by.

sanitary conditions among the squatters sparked a plague, probably bubonic, that destroyed nearly a third of the entire population before it had run its course.

In one respect this heavy death toll must have come as a relief, since Athens's most pressing problem had long been too many mouths to feed; but it also struck a near-lethal blow at the city's moral stability. The epidemic at its height brought about an almost total abandonment of moral standards, a spiraling descent into anarchy and chaos. Physical recovery was fast enough once the disease had run its course, but for the younger generation (and, indeed, for many of their elders) traditional moral standards had been virtually annihilated in the process. This trend was encouraged and even accelerated by the presence in Athens of the Sophists, itinerant teachers who offered courses in the various subjects explored by secular research. They taught mathematics, they expatiated on the nature of matter and the universe; and — above all — they gave instruction in the art of persuasive discourse, presenting oratory and logic as forensic tools with which to advance any opinion.

Here was another momentous revolution. Since time immemorial, all Greek art and literature had embodied an element of what we might term moral, religious, and civic propaganda. It was exhortatory. To make men better was regarded as one of the artist's first duties. By preaching a kind of neutralism, the Sophists cut at the very root of this concept. Furthermore, they found a ready audience. Attacks on religious traditionalism had been a frequent phenomenon for several decades, largely encouraged by Pericles's intellectual circle. Anaxagoras, for instance, caused much annoyance among the pious by arguing that the sun was a lump of molten metal rather larger than the Peloponnese. Such notions were further disseminated, in dilute form, by Euripides, who enjoyed loading his plays with iconoclastic bombshells of every sort. War and plague between them noticeably advanced this trend, leading some to observe that there was more than one kind of pestilence in fifth-century Attica, with the intellectual sort possibly doing the most damage. Or so it seemed to Athens's religious conservatives, who retaliated by initiating a series of heresy trials that would have done credit to seventeenth-century New England.

Pericles died of the plague in 429, and the age he had come to symbolize died with him. Politically, a tougher line was taken almost at once, for Cleon, Pericles's successor as leader of the radical-populist group, was a very different sort of man. He had made his money in tanning, and he thus understood economics and finance in crudely practical terms. Among other things he imposed a capital tax, doubled or even tripled the tribute rate, set up special boards of collectors to extract that tribute from Athens's subject-allies, recommended wholesale genocide as the punishment for Mytilene when that island revolted, and was largely responsible for the Spartan debacle on Sphacteria. As a militarist, Cleon was both more aggressive and more successful than Pericles. By this time, however, the Athenian people had become profoundly war-weary, and consequently after both Cleon and Sparta's most hawkish general, Brasidas, were killed in the same action, both sides hastened to open peace negotiations. The treaty, finally ratified in 421, was named after Nicias, Athens's chief representative at the conference table. Its terms, which resolved nothing, merely gave the contestants a brief respite before the inevitable resumption of hostilities.

Although the years following Pericles's death saw considerable work done on the Acropolis, the scope and emphasis of the program underwent a great deal of modification. The Propylaea, as we have seen, never reached completion — in itself a significant fact. When building resumed around 427 (perhaps to commemorate the Athenian admiral Phormio's naval victories in the Gulf of Corinth), the project undertaken was of a quite different nature and a good deal more modest: the exquisite little temple to Athena Nike that Callicrates had designed some twenty years earlier. Equally significant, when a new temple was undertaken to commemorate the peace of 421, it was associated with those archaic precincts at the north edge of the rock.

Callicrates's simple yet elegant shrine certainly eschewed all hubristic pretensions. It stood on the site of an earlier precinct, also sacred to Athena Nike, and the cult statue it housed — war helmet in one hand, pomegranate of fertility in the other — had been dutifully copied from an ancient wooden image preserved in situ. The new temple's plan was a simple one; a square cella with four Ionic columns at front and back and two entrance pillars flanked by bronze grilles.

Perched on the great southwest bastion, flanking the Propylaea, this little temple was one of the first buildings to catch a visitor's eye. Its subsequent archaeological history is curious. In 1686, the Turks dismantled it to make room for a gun emplacement. The blocks were then built into other new fortifications above the Beulé Gate. In 1835–36, aided by eighteenth-

century drawings of a similar temple (designed by Callicrates and erected on the banks of the nearby Ilissus
River), archaeologists made a laudable, if not entirely
accurate, reconstruction. Just before World War II the
dilapidated bastion was extensively repaired, and the
opportunity was taken to rebuild the shrine a second
time, eliminating previous errors.

After the Peace of Nicias, and perhaps at Nicias's
own instigation, a plan was approved to house Athens's
two great tutelary deities, Athena and Poseidon —
along with such Athenian nymphs and folk heroes as
Erechtheus, Cecrops, Boutes, and Pandrosos — in one
splendid complex, a building known today as the
Erechtheum. The religious stipulations and restric-
tions attached to each of these ancient figures and to
their respective holy precincts posed special problems
for the architects, and the ingenious way in which they
contrived to carry out a nearly impossible commission
deserves considerable respect.

With at least five shrines to be accommodated in one
edifice — and two irregular precincts to be left un-
covered outside — even the Athenian gift for brilliant
improvisation must have been somewhat strained. The
temporary baldachin that had covered Athena's olive-
wood image since the Persian Wars had to be included.
So did Poseidon's saline spring and trident mark. Cecrops's supposed tomb had to remain undisturbed; as
did the enclosure of Pandrosos, with its gnarled and
sacred olive tree. Room had to be found for such hallowed bric-a-brac as a wooden image of Hermes, a fold-
ing chair said to have been made by Daedalus, and
sundry museum items relating to the Persian wars. To
make matters still more difficult, there was almost a

*Named for the junoesque women of Karyai in
Laconia, the caryatids stand in silent regimentation
on the south side of the Erechtheum. They are
near-perfect reflections of the sense of order and
self-restraint that characterized Athens during
the first phase of the Peloponnesian War.*

nine-foot difference in elevation between the northwest and southeast foundations, and this slope was not blocked out. When we recall that the Erechtheum was later converted, with more zeal than delicacy, into a Christian church, and afterward housed a Turkish harem, it is not hard to see why some of the details of its original design are still debated by modern scholars.

Basically, the Erechtheum consists of a four-chambered building with six Ionic columns as its eastern end, framing the main entrance. This building is flanked on the north by a porch sacred to Poseidon and by the altar and precinct of Zeus, and on the south by the justly famous Caryatid Porch with its maidenpillars. Immediately to the west lay the tomb of Cecrops, with Athena's sacred olive beyond it. The easternmost of the four chambers contained the goddess's olive-wood image draped in its woven robe. Before the image stood a golden lamp. This lamp, which had a chimney in the form of a bronze palm tree, was equipped with an asbestos wick and needed refilling only once a year — a not excessively onerous task entrusted to certain elderly widows. Somewhere, perhaps in the west annex, dwelt the sacred serpent, avatar of earthborn Erechtheus himself, which was fed on honeycakes and functioned as "guardian of the house." We might know a good deal more about the significance of the Erechtheum if the frieze that once ran around it had not been so totally shattered that its theme is now past determination.

The contrast between the Parthenon and the Erechtheum scarcely needs emphasis. In the latter, triumphant imperialism has given way to old-fashioned conformist piety, civic self-assertion to religious modera-tion, splendid extravagance to respectable thrift, and mathematical symmetry to the haphazard requirements of ancient and arbitrary cult practice. If the Parthenon crystallizes Pericles's ambitious intellectual world, the Erechtheum hints at a resurgence of something older and perhaps more enduring — devout, middle-of-the-road conservatism. No one better exemplified this latter trend than Nicias, the cautious, respectable statesman who had labored so hard to reach an accord with Sparta. Dilatory and superstitious, Nicias personified the reaction toward tradition and conformity that had been steadily gaining ground during the course of the Archidamian War.

The reversion that Nicias exemplified was far from universal, however. It should rather be regarded as one aspect of the polarizing trend that after 421 tended to divide Athens into irreconcilable groups of die-hard extremists — military adventurers versus dedicated pacifists, democrats versus authoritarians. The very antithesis of Nicias was found in Pericles's ward Alcibiades, a handsome, spendthrift, sexually dissolute young man who was Socrates's favorite pupil and whose passion for racehorses was only equaled by his burning political ambitions. During the next few years these two men personified the conflicting trends in Athenian public life. While Nicias made lavish religious offerings on Delos, Alcibiades won prizes with his chariot teams at the Olympic Games. While Nicias toiled to keep the peace, Alcibiades's diplomatic intrigues with Argos brought Athens and Sparta to the very brink of war.

An open showdown between these two incompatible public figures came in 415, when a proposal, strongly advocated by Alcibiades, was made to launch a major

expedition against Sicily. Motives, as usual, were mixed.
A diplomatic excuse for the foray was at hand in the
form of an appeal for help from the remote Sicilian
town of Segesta. The main objective, however, was
quite simply plunder — grain, timber, cattle, mercenaries, and slaves. The conquest of Sicily, moreover,
could prove a stepping-stone to further acquisitions in
Spain and Carthage. With the wealth and military
resources thus acquired, Athens would eliminate
Sparta, take over the Peloponnesian League, and rule
as undisputed mistress of the Aegean — or so Alcibiades
and his supporters argued. Such a scheme proved irresistible, and when Nicias prophesied disaster the Assembly promptly appointed him joint commander —
with Alcibiades — of the expeditionary force.

The invasion of Sicily began in June of 415. Seldom
in history has an undertaking of this sort been so thoroughly botched through incompetence, carelessness,
and lack of adequate leadership. A scandal involving a
blasphemous parody of the Eleusinian Mysteries led to
Alcibiades's formal impeachment while he was in
Sicily; and he subsequently deserted to Sparta, where
he gave the government some diabolically good advice
on how to destroy his erstwhile countrymen. Nicias
procrastinated outside Syracuse until his initial advantage was completely lost, and a second expedition,
sent out to reinforce the first, suffered a disastrous
defeat. Further delays followed, culminating in the
superstitious commander's refusal to pull out when he
could have done so because the retreat would have
come during an eclipse of the moon. In September 413,
the survivors were massacred by Syracusan troops while
attempting to retreat overland. Hundreds of ships and

thousands of trained men were lost, and the financial and morale cost proved incalculable.

Three years earlier Athens's high-riding imperialists had ruthlessly massacred every citizen on the neutral island of Melos — thus provoking Euripides's famous attack on war atrocities, *The Trojan Women*. Now they faced the very real threat of suffering similar treatment themselves. Soon after the destruction of the Sicilian expeditionary force, the Spartans once more invaded Attica, this time establishing a permanent outpost at Decelea. Faced with such a crisis, the Athenians' first thoughts were of financial retrenchment. All building activity on the Acropolis ceased at once, and panicky officials melted down some of the gold and silver vessels from the temples to raise cash for a new fleet. They even dipped into Pericles's hitherto-sacrosanct 6,000,000-drachma reserve fund. Perhaps most significant of all, a committee of public safety was appointed to "advise" the Assembly — a break with democratic procedure that hinted at trouble to come.

The war was now entering its third and final stage. For years both sides had been doing their best to obtain financial support from Persia. In 411 Sparta finally managed to do so, and this diplomatic shift, which enabled the Spartans to build an adequate fleet, was instrumental in securing Athens's downfall. Politically the period was characterized by violent extremism on both the left and the right — perhaps an inevitable consequence of the crushing defeat in Sicily. The introduction in the Assembly of a scheme to limit the franchise to 5,000 was followed by a full-scale reactionary putsch, carried out while the sailors of the fleet — radical populists to a man — were at Samos.

This crisis, the Revolution of the Four Hundred, broke just after a production of Aristophanes's *Lysistrata*, which contains appropriate allusions to plots and conspiracies. *Lysistrata* also reveals a good deal about both fifth-century Athens and the Acropolis, for its heroines barricade themselves on Athena's rock during their sexual strike against the war.

The play's background is one of profound pessimism, both at home and abroad, of traumatic loss leading to a fear of total collapse. Perhaps that is one reason why the entire action takes place in front of the Propylaea, a continual reminder of the city's past greatness, and upon the great rock with which all of Athens's triumphs and beliefs were so closely bound up. Characteristically, one of the main complaints leveled against Lysistrata and her associates by the chorus of Athenian men is that they have seized the goddess's sacred image, the olive-wood totem. The oath taken by Lysistrata follows an appeal to Peitho, goddess of persuasion, who shared a shrine with Aphrodite Pandemos on the southwest corner of the Acropolis.

After five days of celibacy, some of the women weaken and try to escape from their self-imposed isolation on the Acropolis by any secret exit they can find. Lysistrata catches one of them knocking a hole in the parapet above the north face with the intention of scrambling down past the Cave of Pan — just as the Persians, some seventy years before, had scrambled up. In fact, Aristophanes deploys the whole of the western end of the Acropolis as a familiar backdrop, one that each member of his audience must have seen clearly in his mind's eye. The here and now are never far beneath the surface in *Lysistrata*. Behind the erotic high

jinks lurks the threat of imminent revolution — and only a few months after the first production, fantasy was eclipsed by fact.

The swing toward totalitarian violence in politics, duly foreseen and analyzed by Thucydides, formed only one aspect of the general retreat from reason that characterized the progress of the Peloponnesian War. Such a phenomenon is, of course, perennial. Pliny, the Roman encyclopedist, pointed out that the Peloponnesian War, as well as the Persian wars, was marked by gross outbursts of superstition. Daniel Defoe, in his *The Journal of the Plague Year,* made a very similar observation. It was, then, only to be expected that as the conflict dragged grimly on the Erechtheum would attract more instinctive devotion than that large and rational display piece, the Parthenon. Secularism — always a surface growth — soon lost ground to mana and magic. Erechtheus, snake-tailed Cecrops, and the other fierce demons of death and fertility that still haunted the Acropolis now rose from their uneasy sleep and stalked abroad once more.

The right-wing coup of 411 did not survive for long, but it did have some interesting and unforeseen consequences. Among the more surprising was the rehabilitation of that mercurial figure, Alcibiades. Since his desertion in Sicily, Alcibiades's career had been, to say the least, checkered. Forced to leave Sparta posthaste after seducing King Agis's wife, he had sailed for Ionia, where he soon transferred his allegiance to the local Persian satrap. Next, playing upon his well-known charisma for all it was worth, he managed to get himself elected commander in chief of the Athenian democrats serving with the fleet at Samos. The sailors, with

that flair for internecine warfare so characteristic of Greeks in a crisis, wanted to sail for Piraeus and oust the junta by force. Alcibiades had the presence of mind to stop them — for which action, he later reminded the Assembly, he deserved the gratitude of his country.

Despite the opportunism that clearly dictated his public actions, Alcibiades had a passionate love-hate relationship with Athens, and he even seems to have convinced himself that his treachery had been forced upon him by unscrupulous political opponents. He was determined to return in glory, his past forgiven; but to achieve this end he knew that he must come bearing gifts. For three years he ranged the eastern Aegean, scoring a remarkable series of naval victories over the Peloponnesian fleet and playing an intricate game of double bluff with the Persians. In Athens, the moderate oligarchy fell and democracy was restored, but still Alcibiades bided his time. For one thing, he had been condemned to death in absentia for treachery and blasphemy, and he had been officially cursed by the Athenian priesthood. Somehow that curse had to be lifted; somehow Alcibiades must present himself as not merely patriotic but pious. Toward this end, and to celebrate his victory off Cyzicus in 410, he is thought to have commissioned a marble parapet, topped by a bronze screen and adorned with sculptures, to be set up around the platform on which the Temple of Athena Nike stood. The reliefs showed a celebratory feast, with winged Victories ordering sacrifice to Athena.

A year later, after further naval successes, enough optimism had been generated at Athens to allow a resumption of work on the Erechtheum. Commissioners were appointed to report on the building's progress,

note what remained outstanding, supervise further construction work, and make an inventory of material on the site. All this they did in painstaking detail, and from several lengthy surviving inscriptions we know a good deal about the completion of this last, great classical edifice to be built on the Acropolis. Citizens, slaves, and resident aliens all worked on the project, and for the same wages. The average daily pay was one drachma, and much of the sculpture was paid for on a piece basis. Under a supervisory architect, dozens of specialists carried out their various tasks. There were columns to be fluted, gable-blocks to be shaped, rosettes to be first modeled in wax and then carved from wood. Clerks were needed to keep accounts and inventories, laborers to lay tiles, shift scaffolding, and handle block and tackle. These precious inscriptions provide a first-hand glimpse of the •infinite complexity of temple building in antiquity.

While this work went on, Athens made her last, desperate bid for victory. In 407 Alcibiades finally came home, garlanded with successes, to be greeted by a cheering crowd at Piraeus. He was the last link with the old days of Periclean greatness; somehow, like a talisman, he would work miracles. His lands were restored, and the curses against him rescinded. With one eye on his public image as a devout citizen, he deployed his patrols along the eleven-mile road to Eleusis so that the procession of the Mysteries could once again be held without fear of Spartan attacks. But this orgy of emotional reconciliation lacked effective depth, and after a few weeks the Athenians, having appointed Alcibiades commander in chief once more, sent him out to win the war. They omitted the money without which

victory was impossible, but this was hardly their fault. They had been reduced to melting down gold Victories and issuing coins of silver-plated copper. To raise funds to conduct his campaign against the Spartans, Alcibiades was compelled to waste much of his time winning booty, and one minor defeat suffered by his deputy commander swung the volatile Athenians against their former idol. Alcibiades failed to secure reelection as general, and rather than come back and face probable prosecution he retired to his castle on the Dardanelles and took no further part in the war.

Another Athenian fleet was somehow built from the proceeds of melted-down temple dedications — Athens's last, flimsy wooden wall. She was ill-equipped for any serious military challenge, and she was utterly unprepared for the action taken by Cleophon, the last in a long line of increasingly extremist demagogues who had ruled Athens since 429. Swaggering into the Assembly drunk, he contemptuously rejected Sparta's final offer of a negotiated peace. Slaves were promised their freedom and resident aliens citizenship if they would row in the fleet. Hysteria ran through Athens like wildfire. A successful action was fought off the Arginusae Islands — and the victorious admirals then found themselves prosecuted for failing to pick up survivors in a bad storm. But Athens's last squadrons were defeated at Aegospotami, and in April, after a grim winter's siege, the city surrendered. "After this," Xenophon wrote, "Lysander [the Spartan commander] sailed into Piraeus, the exiles returned, and the Peloponnesians with great enthusiasm began to tear down the walls to the music of flute-girls, thinking that that day was the beginning of freedom for Greece."

VI

THE ROAD TO ROME

Lysander's troops now garrisoned the Acropolis, and statues of him were placed beside those of the gods at Delphi. With Spartan backing and approval, a totalitarian junta known as the Thirty Tyrants took over the government of Athens and proceeded to carry out extensive purges. Resistance to their excesses soon hardened, and after a ferocious three-cornered civil war between ultras, moderates, and populists, democracy was finally restored in 403 and Sparta withdrew her occupying forces from Athens. The scars of that internecine conflict took many years to heal, and the political gulf between what may loosely be called the left and the right in Athens became wider than ever. Both sides took increasingly extreme positions, and as democracy grew more arbitrary and hysterical, respect for the unwritten laws diminished. The Assembly showed an alarming inclination to rule by fiat rather than through legislation, so that in effect the people became both the source and the judge of all law.

It was in this atmosphere that the trial and condemnation of Socrates took place in 399. Socrates's intellectual challenge to cherished traditional assumptions had caused alarm as well as irritation, for the recently defeated city-state, stripped of all imperial pretensions, was clinging to its past with exaggerated fervor. Indeed, there was talk in fourth-century Athens of returning to the ancestral constitution — to idealized, predemocratic rule, to the world of aristocratic tradition and authority that had existed before Solon's day. Authoritarianism was coming into fashion with intellectuals, as Plato's *Republic* makes all too clear. Nor is it hard to see why; the populist excesses of the *demos* alone would suffice to explain such a trend.

This period of political regression was accompanied by an outburst of luxury and individualism in private life. A florid style characterizes early fourth-century art, and it is surely no accident that the favorite mythic figures of the era were Dionysus and Aphrodite. Sensuality and alcohol, those two age-old psychological anodynes, now came to the fore, heralding what historians more soberly label the Age of Individualism. One intriguing symptom of this age was its faintly morbid preoccupation with death, evinced by the elaborate funerary monuments that began to appear in Athens. Typical of this trend is the cenotaph of Dexileos, which stands at the corner of the Street of the Tombs. The fallen warrior's quadrant-shaped monument bears a stele that shows him riding down an enemy, and it is adorned at either end with sirens playing lyres.

Toward the end of the Peloponnesian War, the rear chamber of the Older Parthenon — patched up and still in use as a treasury — was destroyed by fire and rebuilt, and was finally pulled down half a century later. The same conflagration also caused damage to the Erechtheum which, as we know from an inscription, underwent repairs in 395. This building activity must have involved substantial sums of money, and it is undoubtedly true that fourth-century Athens — like many defeated nations temporarily sidetracked from militarism — was enjoying a commercial boom. International trade flourished as never before, and lawyers grew fat on civil cases. Before long, military ambitions revived, and in 394 the Athenian admiral Conon secured a détente with Persia. The result was that only a decade after they' had been pulled down, the Long Walls were rebuilt — and with Persian gold.

In 386, the Great King of Persia virtually dictated a peace treaty to the quarreling Greek states. That same year the Athenian Assembly passed a law stipulating that one play by Aeschylus, Sophocles, or Euripides was to be revived annually. The *polis* was rapidly becoming a nostalgic anachronism. Yet no one, least of all the citizens of Athens, could see this development at the time, or for many years to come.

One astonishing thing about fourth-century Athenians was how little they learned from their too-costly failures. With vast energy and remarkable resilience they set out to build another fleet and another empire along the lines of those they had lost. The old formula was to be refurbished — this time, it was hoped, with greater success. For a time it looked as though their goal might well be achieved. A navy larger than any Athens had possessed in Pericles's day recaptured various lost outposts of empire in the Aegean, and while Sparta and Thebes struggled for supremacy on the mainland, Athens continued to consolidate her position at sea. But after a few years Athens's new maritime empire began to encounter setbacks, and all the Greek states alike failed to reckon with one crucial factor: Macedon — crude, backward, venal Macedon — which was about to emerge as the strongest power in the Balkans.

This extraordinary metamorphosis was due almost entirely to one man, King Philip II. From 359, when he ascended the throne, until his assassination in 336, Philip devoted his full energies to strengthening Macedon's position as a major power. He reorganized the army along Theban lines, and he exploited the gold and silver mines of Thrace to provide a solid national income. Through a characteristic blend of military skill

During the middle decades of the fourth century B.C. the
energy, ambition, and cunning of two men—King Philip II
of Macedon and his son Alexander—were to transform
the backward Balkan province into a world empire second
to none. Divided against themselves, the Greek states were
unable to mount an effective defense against the
Macedonians, and in 338 they lost a decisive battle to
Philip's troops and Alexander's cavalry. Five years later
Alexander engaged Darius III of Persia in battle. That
conflict, but one phase of an extraordinary military
campaign that was to carry the young commander to the
banks of the Indus River in less than a decade, is the
subject of the mutilated mosaic below, which shows the
beardless Macedonian at left, his well-guarded Persian
adversary in a war chariot at right. The remarkably similar
profiles of Alexander and his mother, Olympias, are
paired on the onyx cameo at far right.

and shrewd, if underhanded, diplomacy he expanded his frontiers and holdings at the expense of other Greek states. These he played off against one another with cool, Machiavellian cynicism, exploiting their differences and corrupting their politicians. Demosthenes, the great Athenian orator, attacked Philip repeatedly in his speeches, urging the Athenians to face this threat before it overwhelmed them. Not until it was too late, and Philip had already established himself in central Greece, did Athens and Thebes patch together a strained defensive alliance against him. In 338, the Greek allies — dangerously short on both military training and experience — fought Philip at Chaeronea on the Boeotian plain, where they were decisively defeated. The battle was largely won by Philip's eighteen-year-old son, Alexander, who led a decisive cavalry charge at the critical moment and saved his father's life.

Chaeronea was the graveyard of the free city-state. Thereafter, both Philip and Alexander went out of their way to soothe the touchy Greeks, even going so far as to create a Hellenic league — to which, when it suited them, they would defer. But effective power lay with the Macedonians and their successors. After Philip's assassination, Alexander took over his father's projected expedition against the Persian Empire — ostensibly in revenge for Xerxes' invasion of Greece; in fact, from pure lust of conquest and discovery. Alexander's legendary campaign from the Hellespont to India, his unbroken string of victories, his premature death from fever or poison in Babylon — all events that the modern world tends to view in a context of epic grandeur — the Greeks saw as the excesses of a detested megalomaniac. When news of Alexander's death reached Athens, one

well-known orator scoffed, "Alexander dead? Impossible — the whole earth would stink of his corpse."

On his deathbed Alexander remarked, with prescient irony, that there would be great funeral games when he was gone. And indeed, after an initial partition of territory among his surviving marshals, a bloody and ruthless power struggle did begin. It lasted for some forty years, and of all the king's senior officers only Antipater, viceroy of Greece, died in his bed. In 310, after a flurry of dynastic murders, Alexander's direct line became extinct and the empire he had carved out was, in every sense, up for grabs. By 287 it had been divided among three main dynasties, the Antigonid, the Seleucid, and the Ptolemaic, which were based, respectively, in Europe, Asia, and Egypt. These kingdoms are known as those of the Diadochi, or Alexander's Successors, and they span the Hellenistic Age, which lasted from Alexander's death in 323 until the absorption of the last Successor Kingdom, that of Ptolemy, in 31 B.C. following the defeat of Cleopatra and Mark Antony at Actium.

"Great are the proofs which we have provided," Pericles had declared, "and not unwitnessed is our power, and we shall be the marvel of the present day and of ages yet to come." Indeed, before the rise of Philip fourth-century Athenians still lived in hope of recapturing the proud glories of that brief but immortal ascendancy; their attempt to create a new sea empire offers striking proof of this. But the moment of creative greatness had passed. When Demosthenes invoked his countrymen's "undying possessions," he referred to "the *memory* of their achievements" and "the beauty of the *memorials* set up in their honor — yonder Propylaea, the Parthenon, the porticoes, the docks." He

not only invoked the Parthenon in a wholly secular context, he emphasized the past, not the present, throughout. It was not long before statues of Aeschylus, Sophocles, and Euripides were erected at public expense, and copies of their works were deposited in the state archives. Athens was already well on the way to becoming a museum culture, living on overdrawn Periclean capital. Golden crowns of victory were still deposited in the Parthenon from time to time — but they took their place alongside the tablet commemorating the Great King's peace.

Demosthenes called upon Athens to fight for liberty to the bitter end, but many less committed citizens found a mouthpiece in the orator and educator Isocrates, who preferred collaboration with Philip. Demosthenes prevailed, and as a result Athenian freedom went down before the long pikes of the Macedonian phalanx at Chaeronea. Though given privileged treatment and technically still autonomous, Pericles's violet-crowned city now became, in effect, a satellite of Macedon. The most notable addition to the Parthenon's treasures during this period was a row of gilded shields, dedicated by Alexander himself and hung in a prominent position along the architrave. The young king's Bactrian wife, Roxana, later sent offerings to Athena Polias, indicating that although Athens's political status was shaky, her cultural ascendancy still inspired respect.

Even now, Athenians dreamed of regaining their lost freedom. Urged on by Demosthenes's impassioned diatribes, they set about building up their military and naval reserves once more. Under an austere statesman named Lycurgus, who consciously modeled himself on

Pericles, they raised the city's annual income to some 7,200,000 drachmas, constructed new arsenals and dockyards, overhauled the training program for hoplites, and constructed a standing fleet of between three and four hundred triremes. In 331, Agis III of Sparta revolted against Macedonian overlordship during Alexander's absence, but he was defeated by the viceroy Antipater. The Athenians — perhaps not altogether sorry to see Sparta thus crippled — held aloof from the Peloponnesian rising and waited another eight years, until Alexander's death, before staging their own revolt. They gave Antipater some unpleasant moments at first, but their initial victories were followed by final defeat at Crannon in 322.

The battle of Crannon rang the final death knell for genuine Athenian democracy, which had always drawn its economic strength from seaborne commerce and its political support from the sailors who manned the fleet. The end of one spelled destruction for the other; from then on Athens became a kind of de facto plutocracy, dependent on the goodwill of alien rulers. Freed from the expensive burdens imposed on them by imperialism, Athens's wealthy young men turned to profitable businesses, personal relationships, courtesans, philosophy, haute cuisine, and drink — a private rather than a public world, one duly reflected, somewhat later, in the comedies of such playwrights as Menander.

Loss of political and military preeminence had its compensations, however. Athens was still an enormously prestigious city, a prize for any monarch, and the goal of all scholars, thinkers, and artists. Athenian chefs were famous, and Athenian courtesans fetched astronomic prices. On the other hand, the cost of living rose steeply and, because wages did not always keep up, the gap between rich and poor widened perilously.

The struggle between Alexander's marshals in Greece eventually brought Antipater's son, Cassander, to power. In 318, Cassander appointed an aristocratic reactionary named Demetrius of Phaleron as absolute ruler of Athens. This ex-student of Aristotle and Theophrastus set about dismantling the apparatus of democracy with zealous enthusiasm: election by lot was abolished, the franchise was severely restricted, and numerous sumptuary laws were passed to curtail private extravagance. Business investment was encouraged, and capitalists were relieved of public financial burdens. Unlike Pericles and Lycurgus, Demetrius avoided ostentatious building schemes, preferring to boost art, science, and letters — which were almost as impressive and much cheaper.

In 307 B.C., Demetrius was removed from office, and Athenian democracy was restored, after a fashion, by another, more famous Demetrius, the son of Antigonus. When father and son entered Athens in triumph, they were hailed as gods by the sedulous populace — who had adopted this particular line of flattery after meeting Alexander's requests for deification. "The other gods," they sang in a hymn especially written for the occasion, "are either far away, or they have no ears, or they do not exist, or they pay no heed whatever to us; but thou art here and we see thee, not in wood, or in stone, but in very truth. We therefore pray to thee." Unblushing utilitarianism could go no further. The Athenians welcomed their saviors as kings as well as gods — and Demetrius duly exercised Zeus-like privileges in Athens.

Following Socrates's trial and execution, his loyal disciple Plato spent twelve years in self-imposed exile. Returning to Athens in 387, he founded the Academy, a school of philosophy that is the subject of the Roman mosaic at left. There he formulated his famous dialogues, among which were discourses on government. In fourth-century Athens, citizens voted by inserting metal ballots (above) into tally boards known as kleroteria *(right).*

Fortunately, the changing military situation soon called Demetrius away again, this time to a protracted — and ultimately unsuccessful — siege of Rhodes that earned him the nickname "the Besieger." His absence enabled his recently displaced rival, Cassander, to score a number of striking successes on the mainland, culminating in the defeat of Athens's naval squadrons and the actual investment of the city. News of the siege led Demetrius to break off the blockade of Rhodes and hurry home with a large fleet and army. In the battle that followed he inflicted a crushing defeat upon Cassander, and he celebrated his triumph by spending the winter of 304 in Athens, enjoying himself as a triumphant god-king should. On his voyage across the Aegean he had quartered himself in the shrine of Apollo on Delos — and in so doing made the elementary discovery that Greek stone temples offered the most spacious, cool, and comfortable living quarters then available. The idea, once acquired, proved irresistible, and Demetrius proceeded to set up house in the back chamber of the Parthenon, where he lived in the company of several notorious whores and a rapacious elderly madam.

When a deputation of scandalized Athenians had the temerity to complain, he reminded them with bland irony that their own act of deification had made him Athena's younger brother, and thus he was entitled to the goddess's hospitality. He then added insult to injury by levying a large sum from the Assembly that was to be turned over to his harem as a soap allowance. The Parthenon became the scene of nightly orgies during which scores of Athenian citizens were exposed to the lustful urges of this crude Macedonian baron. By blatant manipulation of religious requirements, Demetrius even got himself initiated into the Eleusinian Mysteries, thus having the best of both worlds.

There is a curious mutability about the events of this period, a flux and reflux of the fortune that played so large a role in Hellenistic affairs. Demetrius of Phaleron had no fewer than 360 statues of himself put up during his years in office, of which only one — on the Acropolis — survived after his fall, the remainder being melted down for chamberpots. Demetrius the Besieger, who nearly succeeded in getting his portrait and that of his father woven into the Panathenaic robe following his triumph over Cassander in 304, was severely defeated by Cassander's allies at Ipsus in Asia Minor three years later. When news of Demetrius's defeat reached Attica, the Athenians, much relieved, promptly exiled his queen and set up an independent government. Its leader, Lachares, made peace with Cassander and emerged as a thoroughgoing tyrant in his own right. But a year or two later the irrepressible Demetrius was back with a fresh army, and Athens prepared — not for the last time — to stand siege.

Demetrius made no effort to assault the walls; starvation, he calculated, would do his work for him more cheaply. One blockade-runner was caught and crucified; the others took the hint. Lachares continued to hold out stubbornly, however, and when money ran short he melted down the temple offerings. One source tells us that he "stripped Athena naked" by removing the gold plates from Phidias's statue in order to mint coins. As food prices soared, the philosopher Epicurus took to rationing his disciples' beans — and a point was reportedly reached at which two men, father and son, fought for possession of a dead mouse. Seeing that further resistance was hopeless, Lachares slipped away by night and the city surrendered. Demetrius, merciful in victory, helped relieve the famine with an emergency donation of grain, but for the next sixty-five years Athens was to have a foreign garrison, and the record of sieges, party strife, and bloodily suppressed revolts makes melancholy reading. It is not hard to see why Pyrrhus advised the Athenians never again to admit a king within their walls.

Two brief periods of quasi-liberty during the ensuing half-century were no compensation for the fact that Athens was repeatedly ground between the ambitious millstones of Macedon on the one hand and Ptolemaic Egypt on the other. Culturally, the city remained as fashionable as ever, but her flourishing schools of art and philosophy could not compensate for near-total political impotence. Politics, and men, made the *polis*. Even the centers of creativity were shifting elsewhere, to Egyptian Alexandria and Pergamum in Asia Minor, where wealthy monarchs knew the advantages to be derived from enlightened, large-scale art patronage along Periclean lines. Antiochus the Great, that most remarkable of all Seleucid rulers, sent Athens a huge golden aegis, a decorative breastplate with a detachable Gorgon mask, to hang on the Acropolis wall above the theater. And the kings of Pergamum commissioned vast porticoes to be erected around the Agora itself.

However, the most important development during the third century B.C. was not cultural but political — and it arose from Rome's growing involvement in the affairs of the Balkan peninsula. In 216 Hannibal the Carthaginian inflicted a shattering defeat on the Roman legions at Cannae, and Macedon at once sought an alliance with Carthage. As a result, Rome found herself committed to a preventive campaign against Macedon in Greece, a campaign to which many would-be independent Greek cities eagerly flocked. Among Rome's more powerful allies in the Aegean area was Attalus I, king of Pergamum, who celebrated his victory over the Gauls of Asia Minor by erecting a series of ex-voto reliefs on the southern bastion of the Acropolis. These reliefs included obligatory representations of giants and Amazons being routed by the forces of civilization — to which Attalus politely added the Athenian victory at Marathon — and a few dying Gauls.

In 197, the Roman consul T. Quinctius Flamininus defeated Philip V of Macedon in Thessaly, and the following year, at the Olympic Games, he proclaimed that henceforth all Greek cities were to be free and independent — a gesture that sounded magnanimous at the time but acquired ironic overtones in retrospect. (One reason for this policy was to prevent the formation of potentially dangerous federations or leagues.) The plain truth was that Rome had no alternative but to pursue a policy of progressive absorption in Greece. Another attempt at independent expansion, led by Philip's son Perseus, was crushed in 167; and in 148, after another abortive uprising, Macedon finally became a Roman province. From this point on even the pretense of freedom and independence was discarded, and two years later the remaining Greek states were brought to heel. Against a background of social anarchy and desperate last-ditch nationalism, a motley force of freemen and slaves was annihilated by the Romans. Corinth was sacked, and Rome took over the affairs of Greece in toto. Athens retained her titular freedom;

once again her past glories — symbolized by the gleaming temples on the Acropolis — had won her a kind of privileged cultural immunity.

It is in 146 B.C. that the independent political history of Greece effectively terminates, to be resumed only after the Greek War of Independence in 1821–28. The peace that her warring states had been unable to achieve by their own efforts became the responsibility of efficient, if rapacious, Roman provincial governors. Yet it was during this period of enforced inertia that Athens made one last bid for freedom, and as a result suffered devastation so appalling that only the sack by the Herulian Goths in A.D. 267 eclipsed it.

In 88 B.C. Mithridates the Great, king of Pontus in Asia Minor, hearing of Rome's savage and crippling war with her Italian allies, decided on a major breakaway bid in Greece and the Near East. Thousands of Roman settlers and businessmen were murdered in a single night, and Mithridates's envoys went to every Greek city, Athens included, soliciting support for a united stand against Rome. The slogan of this uprising was freedom, independence, and democracy — words that appealed rather more to the populace than to the upper classes and the business community, who were pro-Roman almost to a man. On a tide of proletarian enthusiasm, however, Aristion, Mithridates's Athenian envoy, made himself dictator of the city. The minority found it prudent to keep quiet or get out.

It was not to be supposed that Rome would ignore such a threat. Lucius Cornelius Sulla, a veteran commander who was himself destined to become a notable dictator, was sent out at the head of 30,000 seasoned troops to discipline Mithridates and his allies. Soon after Sulla's departure, his political enemies seized power in Rome, and consequently he was obliged to fight a peculiarly ruthless campaign on every count; his own future, no less than Rome's, depended upon it. Sulla saw at once that Athens and the great port of Piraeus must be his first concern. The Long Walls, which had been abandoned for over a century, had fallen into disrepair. Port and city were thus isolated from each other, and they could be dealt with separately. The Roman commander therefore threw a cordon around the city walls of Athens, where Aristion was established, and then set about the task of assaulting Piraeus, which was held by Mithridates's brilliant Greek general, Archelaus.

This proved a singularly tough assignment. The massive walls, dating from Pericles's day, had been built to resist just such an attack. Sulla's first attempt to storm them with scaling ladders was beaten back, and he was obliged to set about more serious preparations. Siege engines were built from timber cut in the shady groves of Plato's Academy, while stones, timber, and earth from the dilapidated Long Walls were used to build a great mound opposite the fortifications. Archelaus held out by building towers of his own, digging galleries that undermined the Roman earthworks and siege engines, and making sorties against the Roman outposts. Sometimes rival tunnels met and the sappers fought underground by the lurid glare of torches. In the end, Sulla was forced to abandon the idea of carrying Piraeus by assault. Instead, he established a cordon around it, hoping to reduce the port by famine. Next, he turned his attention to beleaguered Athens.

By this time the inhabitants of Athens were in appal-

Allied with King Mithridates, ruler of Pontus in Asia Minor, the citizens of Athens attempted to shake off the oppressive Roman yoke in 88 B.C. The uprising, which was initially popular, lost considerable support when it was learned that Lucius Sulla was leading 30,000 Roman legionaries—some of whom are depicted on the bas-relief opposite—against the city. The hapless Athenians were to fare no better half a century later, allying themselves with Mark Antony against Octavian. The latter's triumph at Actium in 31 B.C. is the subject of the intaglio seen at right, which depicts Octavian as the sea god Neptune.

ling straits. Fifth-column agents in Piraeus regularly sent messages to Sulla to alert him that a food convoy was en route from port to city, and the Romans had no trouble in intercepting and capturing the provisions. As a result, a single bushel of wheat sold on the Athenian market for a thousand drachmas. All edible animals in the city had long since been slaughtered, and people were living on soup made from weeds or boiled shoes. Cannibalism was not unknown — yet at the same time, Aristion and a few chosen companions were living in luxury, feasting and drinking and shouting insults at Sulla from the battlements. (The Roman commander had a hideous facial birthmark about which he was particularly sensitive; his temper can hardly have been improved by hearing himself described as a "mulberry sprinkled with meal.") And although Aristion himself never wanted, he let the sacred lamp before Athena's statue go out for lack of oil, and when the priestess begged him for some grain, he sent her peppercorns.

Sulla, too, had his cynical side. To sustain the expense of the siege, he raided the sacred treasures of Olympia, Delphi, and Epidaurus, remarking blandly that he and his men were soldiers of the gods since it was the gods who paid them. At first Aristion refused even to entertain the idea of surrender, and he greeted a deputation urging this step with a fusillade of arrows. Finally, however, he sent two or three envoys to Sulla — in whose presence they delivered set speeches about Theseus, Marathon, and the glories of Salamis. Sulla listened impatiently for a while and then told them, in his dry manner, that the Roman Senate had sent him to subdue rebels, not learn history. The well-tried appeal to Athens's magnificent past fell on deaf ears.

In the end, it was careless talk that brought about Athens's downfall. Some of Sulla's soldiers, bivouacked outside the Ceramicus, heard two old men criticizing Aristion for his failure to repair a weak stretch in the western fortifications. After reconnoitering the wall himself on March 1, Sulla decided upon a night attack. His rams soon brought down the crumbling masonry, and a horde of legionaries poured through the gap, swords drawn, trumpets blaring, eager for the kill. Sulla had expressly forbidden them to set any buildings on fire, but otherwise his troops were free to loot, rape, and massacre at will. As the historian Appian records, Sulla "was angry that the Athenians had so suddenly joined the barbarians without cause, and had displayed such violent animosity towards himself." The resultant slaughter was appalling; Plutarch notes that "without mention of those who were killed in the rest of the city, the blood that was shed in the Agora covered all the Ceramicus inside the Dipylon Gate: indeed, many say that it flowed through the gate and deluged the suburb." Many Athenians, weakened by famine, killed themselves or deliberately ran upon the unsheathed swords of their assailants.

At the urging not only of the Athenian exiles but also of the Roman officers on his own staff, Sulla finally called a halt to the indiscriminate slaughter, remarking that he "forgave a few for the sake of many, the living for the sake of the dead." It may also have occurred to him that live prisoners brought in money, whereas corpses were merely so much carrion.

As Sulla's soldiers entered Athens, Aristion and a few of his followers barricaded themselves on the Acropolis, burning Pericles's concert hall, the Odeum, as they

115

went in order to prevent Sulla from using its timbers for siege engines. Starvation and lack of water soon forced them to capitulate, however, and they were executed without mercy. Immediately after their surrender, a spring cloudburst deluged the city, filling every cistern. This was regarded as a sign from heaven condemning the insurgents.

Despite the depredations of his predecessors, Sulla managed to remove forty pounds of gold and six hundred pounds of silver from the shrines on the Acropolis. Athens had been subjugated — but Piraeus still held out against Sulla's encircling troops. Finding himself unable to dislodge Archelaus from his stronghold without a fleet, Sulla set the great port on fire, reducing it to ashes — docks, navy yard, arsenals, and all. (Twenty centuries later, workmen digging a trench in modern Piraeus found four magnificent bronze statues that are thought to be part of Sulla's loot, accidentally left behind in a warehouse at the time of the great conflagration.) As a parting gesture, the Roman commander deprived Athens's surviving citizens of the right to vote or hold elections for the rest of their lifetimes. The insult was a well-chosen one, even if the privilege itself was by then almost meaningless.

"After 86 B.C.," it has been well said, "resignation was the only policy for the Athenians; meekness their cardinal virtue." But there was one last act to be played in the ancient Greeks' drama of resistance, one final savior upon whom they were to pin their hopes. The convulsive civil wars that marked the close of the Roman republic were largely fought on Greek soil — at Dyrrhachium, Pharsalia, and Philippi. Moving through them was that strangely attractive soldier and debau-

chee, Mark Antony, whose romantic charisma nowhere proved more potent than in Athens. The Athenians welcomed him as a new Dionysus — the comparison with Alexander the Great was obvious — and they even offered him Athena as a bride in a religious ceremony full of ritual symbolism. Antony not only accepted the espousal, but relieved the city coffers of a 6,000,000-drachma dowry. Like Demetrius the Besieger he conducted fantastic bacchanals on the Acropolis — during which so many lamps twinkled from the temple roofs that they lit up all Athens. And when he set out on his Parthian campaign Antony took with him a sprig from Athena's sacred olive tree.

Who could resist so stylishly sensuous a soldier of fortune? Certainly not the Athenians, who cheerfully threw in their lot with Antony — just as they had thrown in their lot with Brutus and Cassius a short time before. They even accepted his mistress, Cleopatra, confident that the two would make short work of Antony's sickly and despotic rival, Octavian. The gods chose otherwise, signifying their displeasure by blowing down the lovers' statues from the Acropolis. The battle of Actium left Greece in Octavian's coolly capable hands and destroyed the last Hellenistic kingdom, Ptolemaic Egypt. Athens's future role under Rome was to be that of a modest though distinguished cultural backwater, a university town where Roman youths were sent to acquire some cosmopolitan polish before plunging into the real business of life. The last obsequies of the Greek city-state had been celebrated, leaving behind a museum without walls. Few could have foreseen its strange and artificial resurrection almost two millennia later.

VII

METAMORPHOSIS AND REVIVAL

Octavian's first visit to Athens was a brief one, during which he arranged for emergency grain supplies, deprived the city of the lucrative perquisite of selling honorary citizenship to aspiring foreigners, had himself initiated into the Eleusinian Mysteries, and then retired, aloof as always, to Aegina. Greece as a whole, however, enjoyed special privileges under Octavian and his successors. Augustus, as he was later entitled, separated Greece proper from Macedon and turned it into the province of Achaea. The capital of this province was not Athens but Corinth, the commercial city par excellence that had been rebuilt in 44 B.C., a century after its sack by Mummius. It is significant that though the emperors and many wealthy private patrons lost no time in restoring or augmenting Athens's cultural amenities, her fortifications were left largely in ruins. Athens had the Pax Augusta to protect her, and any refortification scheme was frowned upon by the Romans; it would only encourage thoughts of rebellion.

Indeed, the whole fabric of civic government as it had been understood in Pericles's day became an elaborate sham under the Roman Empire. Athens still elected archons and generals, but these offices were now empty honors. In Rome itself, the rank of senator, the very consulship, came to mean less and less as time went on. True power lay with the emperor and his Greek-run civil service. As a result, the intellectual elite everywhere retreated into a sterile private world of exotic scholarship, academic philosophy, formalized rhetoric, obscure mythological allusions, and complex personal poetry. Public flattery of the great was matched by private agonizing over the individual's ego and, increasingly, his soul.

During this period political cynicism found oblique but unmistakable expression in the regular reuse of dedicatory statues for different recipients. One interesting example of this process is the vast chunk of gray Hymettus marble, some twenty-nine feet high, that stands immediately below the Propylaea and is commonly known as the Monument of Agrippa. What survives is the plinth, which was designed to support a quadriga. Partially erased inscriptions show that Marcus Vipsanius Agrippa — Augustus's son-in-law and twice consul — was not the original dedicatee. First erected around 174 B.C. in celebration of a chariot victory by one of the Pergamene kings, the plinth afterward bore those statues of Antony and Cleopatra that were toppled by the prophetic hurricane of 31. Agrippa took over the vacant plinth four years later.

Even emperors themselves did not escape this process. Over the years parsimonious Athenian officials managed, by a process of recapitation, to turn Augustus into Tiberius — and then into Nero, Vespasian, and finally Titus. The Acropolis became cluttered with honorific statues and commemorative plaques. A dumpy, circular temple to Rome and Augustus was constructed within twenty yards of the Parthenon — perhaps as a deliberate reminder of political priorities — but all ancient writers pointedly ignore it.

The truth was that from 31 B.C. on, the history of Roman Athens revolved around imperial edicts or visitations. Augustus himself returned in 19, and he is said to have met Vergil on the Acropolis during that stay. (The poet, already in the grip of his last illness, was on his way back to Italy after a leisurely tour during which he had at last nearly finished *The Aeneid*.)

In January of A.D. 18, Tiberius's heir-presumptive, Germanicus, visited Athens and was honored by the usual statue, erected opposite the one of Agrippa on the approach to the Propylaea. (The block employed in this instance had been cut for an equestrian group as early as 457 B.C., and it was unceremoniously turned upside-down to accommodate its new occupant.) Some twenty years later, Claudius — or perhaps Caligula — commissioned a new and splendid flight of marble steps for the Propylaea ramp that was reminiscent of the approach to the capitol in Rome. And in A.D. 67–68 Nero made a triumphant concert tour through Greece, collecting gold crowns at every performance and removing some of the choicer statues from the Acropolis to adorn his Golden House. Trajan, visiting Athens some years later, was hailed as the "benefactor and savior of the world."

The climax of this strange relationship between Athens and the Roman emperors — compounded of flattery, patronage, contempt, and a deeply ingrained romantic nostalgia for past Greek achievements that produced an extraordinary archaizing trend in Roman art — came with the accession of Hadrian. This bearded, bisexual dilettante, with his languorously beautiful boy-lover, Antinoüs, and his devotion to Greek literature and philosophy, expended vast sums of money to restore Athens according to his own mildly baroque vision of the past. Fortunately, he did not meddle with the Acropolis complex. He did complete the vast temple of Olympian Zeus, begun over six centuries earlier by Pisistratus, and he gave the city a gymnasium, a pantheon, and a splendid public library. The arch that bears his name still stands today.

On the side that faces the Acropolis is inscribed "This is Athens, the ancient city of Theseus." On the opposite face is the legend: "This is the city of Hadrian and not of Theseus." Modesty was clearly not one of Hadrian's virtues; indeed, he had an engaging weakness for erecting — or encouraging others to erect — statues of himself wherever he stopped on his travels.

Intellectually sophisticated and with a keen eye for social pretensions, politically impotent but honed to a fine edge by daily exercise in philosophical dialectic and oratorical tropes, the men of Athens whom St. Paul addressed in A.D. 54 must have been a formidable audience. Paul tried to cash in on their superstitious caution by appropriating their Unknown God as his own, but the Stoics and Epicureans were not impressed. Some even seem to have believed that Jesus and Resurrection were yet another Divine Couple. These smart academics and bored matrons may well have snickered at Paul's Cilician accent, or found his urgent zeal a trifle vulgar; yet here, had they known it, was the spearhead of a movement destined to overthrow their philosophies and transform their world. Paul made few converts in Athens, however; no city resisted Christianity as long or with such a sense of intellectual superiority.

Nor were Athenians impressed by mere wealth or ostentation, as the Romans were. Lucian the satirist has left us an acid-tongued account of how his fellow Athenians cut one millionaire down to size by commenting audibly on his pretentious public behavior. The man in question may well have been Marcus Aurelius's friend and tutor, Herodes Atticus, who divided his life between rhetoric and philanthropy but was not above shrewd financial negotiations at the ex-

pense of his fellow citizens. Among other munificent acts of patronage, he rebuilt the Panathenaic stadium with Pentelic marble. Wags observed that "Panathenaic" was a good name for it, since its cost had been defrayed with cash unlawfully abstracted by Herodes from the city as a whole.

The rhetorical movement with which Herodes was connected, known as the Second Sophistic, aimed at ornamental display rather than education. Hadrian had been the first to endow a professorship of sophistics; other such chairs soon followed. Scholarship became progressively more rarified and remote as one emperor succeeded another, although at the same time philosophers developed an unexpected talent for speculating in real estate and living luxuriously. Meanwhile, beyond the frontiers of the empire, barbarian peoples were once more on the move. In 175 a northern tribe pushed south into central Greece, and in about the middle of the third century A.D., after a Gothic incursion reached Salonica, the emperor Valerian ordered his provincial officials to refortify the isthmus and the cities of Greece. Athens duly set about repairing her neglected walls, but a few years later the Herulian Goths, pouring down from the Black Sea area, penetrated Greece's frontier defenses and took Athens. The lower city was sacked and burned in 267, and only the Acropolis survived unscathed.

This disastrous incursion, which saw the end of many public monuments and civic institutions, especially those centered around the Agora, has been rightly characterized as one of the most critical turning points in the entire history of Athens. Such splendid edifices as the concert hall of Agrippa were stripped

Sacked by Sulla and restored to grace by Octavian, Athens entered into a rather curious relationship with Rome, one marked by studied contempt on the one hand and incredible imperial largess on the other. Foremost among Athens's royal patrons was the lascivious Hadrian, who lavished huge sums of money on both restoration projects and new construction. The splendid library erected in his name bears an inscription similar to the one at left, which indicates that the library is open "from the first hour until the sixth." First-century Athens also boasted three public theaters, the oldest constructed by Pericles, the latter two during the Roman occupation. Last and largest of these is the Odeon of Herodes Atticus (below), named for the noted philanthropist who tutored Marcus Aurelius.

No major city in the West resisted Christianity as long or as haughtily as did Athens, and it took a catastrophe as devastating as the sack of the city by the Herulian Goths in A.D. 267 to convert the cynics of Athens to the cause of Constantine. By the first decades of the fifth century it was clear that paganism in Athens was doomed, but many more centuries were to pass before St. George—the patron saint of Greece who is depicted on the icon above—fully replaced Athena. The delicate Byzantine jewelry opposite belongs to this period, an era when the "new Rome" was the strongest influence in the Aegean.

down to their very foundations, and fire damage was extensive. Despite the suddenness of the disaster, the Athenians rose to the occasion with panache. Under a public official named Dexippus, who organized a force of two thousand guerrillas — including the Acropolis garrison — the Athenians drove the Goths out of Attica.

Athens then looked to her defenses — and the city became a fortress once more. Just as Themistocles had conscripted men, women, and children to help build emergency walls in 479 B.C., corvée labor was used again to shape debris from the outer ruins into a new inner defense line enclosing a mere forty acres to the north of the Acropolis. This shrunken perimeter embodied what is now known as the Beulé Gate, directly below the Propylaea, and the Roman market.

For well over a century the area outside this small core was left desolate, a wilderness of broken blocks and columns. The Agora became a rubbish dump for bones, ashes, and household garbage. Yet despite all this, Athens's economic and intellectual recovery was rapid enough. Within fifty years Piraeus was able to provision Constantine's fleet, and Athens's famous philosophical schools never closed.

Synesius, who later became bishop of Ptolemais, visited Athens between 396 and 400. His view of the city was a depressing one, for it was written shortly after a raid by Alaric the Goth had destroyed the Academy. According to Synesius, the city looked like the hide of a sacrificed animal, and all she could boast of were her great past names. Why, this envious Alexandrian asked, should students from Athens put on such lofty airs? To his satisfaction he discovered that "the proconsul has taken away all the pictures from

the Painted Stoa, thus snubbing these men's pretensions to learning. . . . Athens, which of old had been the home of the wise now depends for renown on its beekeepers." No one would guess from Synesius's account that the Acropolis temples still stood in all their undiminished glory.

But decay and condescension can combine to make a powerful irritant — and in this case there was also a religious element involved, for while Athens continued to philosophize in the old Hellenic tradition, Christianity was sweeping through the empire with ever-increasing momentum. Politics and faith merged in Constantine the Great to produce two crucial changes after 330. First, the emperor made Christianity the official state religion; and second, he moved his capital eastward to Byzantium, on the Bosporus, which then became "the city of New Rome which is Constantinople." In the long run, Constantine's first decision spelled doom for the pagan schools of Athens. The second — which came after the final partition of the Roman world into two independent halves, Eastern and Western — created the Byzantine Empire, which survived its Latin counterpart by almost a millennium. Athens was profoundly affected by both changes, although undoubtedly the antipagan legislation did her traditional institutions the most immediate and the most irreparable harm.

In 425, Theodosius II founded the University of New Rome at Constantinople as a Christian counter-attraction to Athens's secular philosophy schools. Ten years later, he issued an edict ordering the destruction of all pagan temples and shrines in the Near East and the purification of their sites by the erection of a cross.

Theodosius's pious fiat was ignored in many areas, however, and nowhere more blatantly than in Athens, which in 400 had begun to experience a revival of prosperity and was in the process of carrying out extensive new building plans near the Agora. The temples somehow survived and philosophers still found a ready audience. The Panathenaic procession continued to be held, and Plutarch, the founder of the Neoplatonic Academy, paid for the transport of the Panathenaic ship, or float, on three separate occasions — a gesture that reportedly cost him his entire fortune. Later edicts earned a stay of execution for the temples, and sometime in the late sixth or early seventh centuries many of them were converted into churches.

Yet quite early in the fifth century Proclus, another distinguished Neoplatonist, foresaw all too clearly that paganism was doomed in Athens. The temples might still stand, but they had been systematically deconsecrated. Phidias's great statue of Athena — along with his Zeus from Olympia and the bronze Athena Promachos that had so impressed Alaric the Goth — had been shipped off to Constantinople. All three eventually perished in fires or riots.

The final blow came in 529 when Justinian closed all the philosophical schools in Athens — a move aimed largely at suppressing the Neoplatonic Academy — and sequestered their funds and endowments. Thus ended a thousand-year tradition of learning. The Academy's revenues had been considerable; Proclus, as its head, had received an annual income of a thousand gold pieces from property that had yielded only three in Plato's day. Thus Justinian's act of closure had more than religious or intellectual significance; at one stroke

The momentous impact of Constantine's conversion to Christianity redounded in all corners of the Eastern Empire, for by his example the emperor—who is sanctified in the Byzantine ivory at left—induced conversion on a massive scale. That tide reached its high point under the emperor Justinian (far right), who closed Athens's philosophical schools in 529. The city's temples were then converted to churches, and crosses (above) were carved into their walls.

it deprived Athens of her main source of income and abolished her international reputation. As a result, the city of Pericles and Plato soon became a stagnant backwater without even serious pretensions to learning.

A new age was dawning, one utterly remote from the splendors of the classical past. Athletics gave way to asceticism, and the noisy Assembly to the remote and hieratic complexities of the Byzantine court. Worse still, from the sixth century onward there were massive incursions of Slav, Avar, and Bulgar tribesmen into the Greek peninsula. Around 580, a horde of 100,000 "Sclavonians" (Slavs) ravaged Thrace and Illyricum, and archaeological evidence shows that they got at least as far south as Athens, where the lower city and the Agora once more suffered widespread devastation. Until the middle of the seventh century squatters hung on amid the ruins, but after that time the outer quarters of Athens were virtually abandoned for almost three hundred years. Moreover, large numbers of these invading tribesmen remained as permanent settlers, and it is clear that during this period the ethnic composition of the Greek people underwent considerable change. A devastating plague in 746, combined with the steady drift of skilled craftsmen to Constantinople, left many areas more or less uninhabited — obvious targets for colonization. During the eighth century the southern Balkans and Greece actually went under the name of Sclavinia.

Yet even then Athens retained certain privileges, and she never seems to have fallen into a total decline even though successive Byzantine administrators regarded Greece as "an utter hole," a place of uncomfortable exile. Athenians could boast that no governor was

allowed to enter their city with an armed force, and that their financial liabilities were limited to land tax, ship money, and the presentation of a gold wreath for each new emperor's coronation. One high official whose exactions proved too irksome was actually stoned to death at the altar of Athens's cathedral church. This edifice, dedicated first to the Holy Wisdom (and later to Our Lady of Athens, the Panaghia Atheniotissa) was none other than the Parthenon in a new guise. Athena the Warrior Maiden had become, or had been replaced by, the Virgin Mother of God.

To accomplish this metamorphosis various structural changes and additions had been necessary. A Christian church by definition faced east, which meant inserting a monumental entrance at the west side of the building. The western cella thus became the narthex, and the eastern chamber became the pronaos. More radical still, the eastern side of the pronaos had to be expanded into an apse to contain the altar. During the reconstruction work that this entailed, the central sculptural group of the east pediment, the one portraying the birth of Athena, was — symbolically enough — removed and destroyed. Lateral windows were pierced through the fabric, and the Doric columns of the peristyle were linked by a low wall. The coffered roof was replaced by ecclesiastical vaulting, and an iconostasis was raised before the altar. The apse was decorated with a mosaic honoring the Panaghia Atheniotissa, and the whole interior was adorned with the usual Byzantine frescoes, some still just visible. For the episcopal throne, a marble chair was brought up from the Theater of Dionysus.

At about the same time the Erechtheum, too, became a Christian church, likewise dedicated to the Mother of God. The zealous builders faced a similar problem here; they had to produce a vaulted basilica with a nave and aisles, a western entrance porch, and an eastern apse. What made their task more difficult in this case — and caused far greater havoc in the interior of the building — was the variation in floor level, which they reduced throughout to that of the central and western sections.

During this same period, the Temple of Hephaestus became the Church of St. George, and the Propylaea — where during the nineteenth century a fresco of SS. Gabriel and Michael came to light — probably did duty as the bishop's palace. Critics who censure these Byzantine church architects for their rough handling of classical material would do well to reflect that without the church's interest these buildings might not have survived at all.

Although eclipsed in commercial terms by cities like Thebes, Athens still held something of its old glamour. In 1018, for example, the Byzantine emperor Basil II repulsed a great Bulgarian invasion in the north. (At the climax of his successful campaign he is said to have blinded some 15,000 prisoners, leaving only one man in a hundred to guide his comrades home.) Known henceforth as Basil the Bulgarslayer, the monarch made a special journey to Athens after his victories, something no Byzantine emperor had done for the past three centuries. He honored the shrine of the Virgin with rich gifts taken from the Bulgar booty, among them a golden dove that fluttered ceaselessly above the high altar. As a quid pro quo the Athenians added Basil's own portrait to the frescoes decorating the Parthenon.

Toward the end of the twelfth century, Athens had the good fortune to receive a bishop who was also a

During the sixth century the austere and solitary Temple of Hephaestus (left) was renamed the Church of St. George, and crosses were incised on its capitals. These superficial changes in no way altered the structure's overall appearance, in form as immutable as the Parthenon itself. Like its famous near-twin on the Acropolis, the Temple of Hephaestus was begun in 449 B.C. and completed during the heyday of Periclean Athens.

first-rate classicist and theologian. Michael Akominatos, brother of the statesman and historian Nicetas, arrived in Athens brimming with classical idealism and Christian zeal, a dangerous mixture. The physical realities of the place shattered him. "Most unhappy city," he exclaimed, "where is your splendor?" He went on to declare that "the entire glory of Athens is passed away; not even a dim trace of it can be seen." The good bishop seems to have neglected his own cathedral, the Parthenon, in this context.

But perhaps what the city lacked its people might yet make good. At his inauguration Bishop Michael preached a vigorous sermon in which he expressed confidence that his flock, as Christians, would inevitably outshine the virtues of their ancestors. Once again rude disappointment awaited him, for the congregation found his classical Greek incomprehensible, and they gaped at him as though he were speaking some foreign tongue. Many spent the service deep in private gossip, and the learned bishop could only shake his head sadly over the Athenians' boorishness. Corruption and ignorance met him everywhere, even among his own clergy, whom he found feeble, illiterate, and litigious. (He was obliged, for example, to rebuke the abbot of Kaisariané Monastery for appropriating other people's bees.) Yet all these things were the merest peccadilloes when set beside the venal rapacity of the imperial tax collectors.

In 1204 the tidal fury of the Fourth Crusade abruptly burst upon this stagnant backwater. Ever since the Great Schism of 1054, which sundered Orthodoxy from Catholicism, many Western powers had turned covetous eyes toward the ramshackle but wealthy Byzantine Empire. And although the Fourth Crusade was

Captured in the course of the Fourth Crusade, the humbled city of Athens endured two and a half centuries of Western rule before falling to the Turks in 1456. By that time a crenelated Frankish tower, visible in the 1670 drawing at near right, had been added to the Acropolis. Its bulk contrasts sharply with the delicacy of the minaret added by the Turks after they converted the Parthenon to a mosque. That spire ironically survived when, in 1687, Venetian artillery detonated a powder magazine housed in the Parthenon (far right).
Overleaf:
The explosion of 1687 shattered Athena's temple and damaged its latter-day additions. Tragically altered, the Acropolis became a kind of open-air museum, drawing artists, poets, archaeologists, and the merely curious.

originally preached to recover Jerusalem from the infidel Turk, the Crusaders found it more politic — and more profitable — to capture Constantinople instead and parcel out its imperial possessions as baronial fiefs. One of these, Attica, fell to a Burgundian named Otho de la Roche.

For the next two and a half centuries Athens was held in turn by Franks, Catalans, and Florentines — and during this period her classical past was almost totally forgotten. The Parthenon, converted to the Latin rite and renamed Notre Dame d'Athénes, was actually thought by the city's gullible and ill-informed citizens to have been built by two sixth-century patriarchs — so much of the glorious past had been forgotten. And when the Italian traveler Niccolò de Martoni was shown around the building in 1390, his main interest centered upon the Christian relics housed there — the skull of St. Macarius, St. Helena's autographed copy of the Gospels. Religious interests aside, the main function of the Acropolis throughout this period was as a fortress. Additional defenses included the famous Frankish Tower, which is familiar from many old engravings and which was not pulled down until 1875.

These years of Western domination have an extraordinarily romantic appeal. Guy de la Roche, the Frankish lord, had himself created duke of Athens by Louis IX, and one of his descendants fought at the great Tournament of Corinth in 1304, the tourney at which seven champions from the West pitted themselves against the knights of the duchy. During Guy's reign, courtly French was spoken in both Athens and Thebes. Troubadours not only flourished but found Greek imitators. This whole courtly world perished in 1311, however, when the flower of Walter de Brienne's Frankish chivalry went down at Orchomenus before the grim mercenaries of the Catalan Grand Company.

For half a century the duchy of Athens endured Catalan rule, nominally under an Aragonese overlord. Pedro IV of Aragon, himself a troubadour, was virtually alone in this period in showing any real aesthetic appreciation of the Parthenon, which he described as "the most precious jewel that exists in the world, and such that all the Kings of Christendom could in vain imitate." His wife, Sybilla, with more conventional piety, showed interest only in the holy relics of Seu de Santa Maria de Cetinas, as the Catalans termed the Parthenon. This contrast of interest recurs in the two key travelers' accounts of the period. Whereas Niccolò de Martoni, like Sybilla, had eyes only for Christian bric-a-brac, Cyriac of Ancona brought with him the new wind of the Italian Renaissance. He visited Athens twice, in 1435 and again in 1444, and on each occasion he copied inscriptions, sketched monuments, and in general devoted himself to the pursuit of antiquity. He saw, among other things, the "noble temple of Pallas," describing it with fair accuracy and enthusing over its pedimental sculptures.

It is no accident that Cyriac's visits coincided with the seventy-odd years of Florentine domination over Athens. Unlike their rude predecessors, the Acciaiuoli family were men of considerable culture and learning. They not only turned the Propylaea into an elegant Renaissance palazzo, they actually treated their Greek subjects on more or less equal terms, a striking innovation. After two centuries of exile, Orthodoxy

was reestablished in the duchy — although the Parthenon remained a Catholic cathedral. The Orthodox metropolitan, perhaps regarding this as a personal slight, repaid Nerio Acciaiuoli's generosity by intriguing with the Turks in hopes of expelling the "schismatic barbarians," as he called the Florentines. By this time ancient Athens had been virtually destroyed, and the surviving ruins were more or less identical to those seen and delineated by such eighteenth-century visitors as Stuart and Revett. Much myth still clung about these antique edifices. The Temple of Olympian Zeus was identified as Hadrian's palace, and the Lysicrates Monument was popularly known as Demosthenes' Lantern to signify the spot where the great orator supposedly wrote his speeches. Although many other equally romantic and farfetched identifications were made during this period, the process of rediscovery had at least begun — and credit for this is undoubtedly due to the enlightened Florentine regime.

Early in the fifteenth century, the Acciaiuoli began to pay tribute to the Turkish sultan. They were the first rulers of the duchy ever to do so, but there were solid reasons behind this decision. For one thing, the Turks had already penetrated the Balkans, occupying Thessaly in 1393 and threatening Constantinople itself — which finally fell in 1453. The Acciaiuoli held on until 1456, when Mohammed II succeeded in deposing them and annexing their duchy. The lower town surrendered at once; the Acropolis held out until 1458. After its capitulation, the sultan himself made a triumphal entry into the city. Mohammed was a far from typical Turkish ruler, one who not only spoke Greek but was well acquainted with Athens's glorious past.

He was also shrewd enough politically to see that the best counterweight to Western influence was the encouragement of Greek Orthodoxy. And thus it was that, on the intervention of a Moslem, Pericles's temple to Athena once more became the seat of a metropolitan, and Greece settled down to nearly four hundred years of Turkish occupation.

Ottoman toleration had its limits, however, and few Turkish rulers were as enlightened as Mohammed. Around 1460, an abortive attempt to restore the duchy led to the Parthenon's final religious transformation — into a mosque. (By this time it had presumably struck the Turkish authorities that Orthodoxy, in addition to providing a bastion against Western influence, could also form the spearhead of national revolt.) The Christian altar was ripped out, the mosaics were plastered over, and whitewash was applied to the frescoes. A minaret was built at the southwest corner of the rear chamber, from which the muezzin could summon the faithful to prayer. The aga made his headquarters in the Propylaea, and used the Erechtheum to house his harem. The Acropolis as a whole received extensive additional fortifications, mostly along the western approaches, until it became a bristling mass of turrets, redoubts, and curtain walls. From this point on, except in special circumstances, it became inaccessible to Christians, and representations of it during this period are few, since anyone sketching the defenses was liable to be arrested as a spy.

Indeed, for some two centuries the record is virtually blank. Only after 1650 does evidence once more begin to accumulate. In 1669, a group of Capuchin friars founded a monastery below the Acropolis on a plot of

land that included Demosthenes' Lantern — which they used to house their library. Travelers from the West began to appear, the most notable of whom were Jacob Spon and George Wheler, who produced the first remotely adequate topographical survey of Athens in 1675. For three *okas* of coffee they bribed their way onto the Acropolis, noting that the night guards "go the Rounds of the Walls, making a great hallowing and noise, to signifie their Watchfulness." They were duly impressed by the Parthenon, "which is not only still the chief Ornament of the Cittadel; but absolutely, both for Matter and Art, the most beautiful piece of Antiquity remaining in the World."

At about the same time, an anonymous Flemish draftsman in the employ of the marquis de Nointel made drawings of the Parthenon sculptures, including both pediments and more than half of the frieze. This proved to be an unbelievably lucky accident for posterity, as an event that occurred almost two decades later was to confirm. In 1683 John III Sobieski, king of Poland, halted the Turks at the very gates of Vienna, and this victory led to the formation of a holy league against the infidel. In September 1687 the Venetians, as league members, overran most of the Peloponnese and besieged Athens. As director of operations they had hired a Swedish field marshal, Count Koenigsmark, who as a student had prepared a Latin thesis lamenting Athens's subjugation by the barbarous Ottomans. This did not prevent him, on September 26, from ordering that a mortar barrage be aimed at the Parthenon in the hope of detonating the Turkish powder magazine emplaced there. One round dropped through a hole in the temple roof. The resultant explosion shattered twenty-eight columns, blew out the walls of the cella, brought down the massive architraves together with large sections of the frieze, and distributed most of the roof over the surrounding countryside. By a kind of supreme irony, the minaret added by the Turks two centuries earlier remained intact.

As a dedicated Hellenophile, Count Koenigsmark expressed sincere regrets over the damage, but he clearly felt that he had done no more than his duty. A fire raged on the Acropolis for two days, and the Turkish garrison finally surrendered. The Venetian commander tried to remove the horses from the west pediment as a souvenir, but the tackle broke as they were being lowered and the statue group was smashed to pieces. By that winter it became clear that the Venetians could not hold Athens, and in 1688 they evacuated the city, taking the Christian minority with them. In retrospect, the entire expedition had been completely pointless. By April 1688 the Turks were once more ensconced on the Acropolis, having cleared the Athena Nike bastion as a gun emplacement. Their garrison did not finally evacuate the fortress until April 12, 1833, by which time the Greek War of Independence was over — and even then they were replaced at once by King Otho's Bavarians.

During the eighteenth and early nineteenth centuries Western interest in Greece increased out of all recognition. Architects studied the monuments; scholars lamented the dilution, with Slav and Albanian stock, of the "pure" Hellenic race; antiquaries, stimulated by the remarkable excavations at Pompeii and Herculaneum, poked about among the broken columns, removing many items of interest; and gentlemen passed through on the grand tour. The Turkish authorities were slothful, philistine, bigoted, and suspicious — but infinitely open to bribes. It began to strike many educated Westerners that the descendants of those demigods, the ancient Hellenes, deserved something better than permanent subjection to such barbarians — who turned ancient monuments into powder magazines or seraglios, and who were not above defacing representations of the human form for the greater glory of Allah. This "freedom movement" received great encouragement from the French Revolution of 1789, which inspired Greek patriots such as Constantine Rhigas and Adamantios Korais to work, mostly abroad, for the cause of Greek independence.

During this same period Lord Elgin, the British ambassador to Constantinople, had obtained a special authorization from the Turks "to take away from the Acropolis any pieces of stone with old inscriptions or figures thereon." He exercised this privilege to the hilt, removing large sections of the surviving frieze, numerous metopes, much pedimental sculpture, and one of the caryatids from the Erechtheum. His booty reached England in 1812, the year that Napoleon invaded Russia, and after much debate in Parliament it was purchased by the British Museum for £35,000. Put on exhibition in 1816, the Elgin Marbles at once became a cause célèbre. Fashionable London dandies adopted a posture known as the "Grecian bend," and Keats sat in contemplation of the sculptures for hours at a time — as he himself stated, like a "sick eagle looking at the sky."

Many critics of the period, imbued with that romantic illogicality so dear to the philhellene, launched broadside attacks against what Byron termed the "rape"

of a precious Greek national heritage. In so doing they ignored both the wanton Turkish indifference to works of art or antiquities and the fact that Elgin's opposite number, the French ambassador Choiseul-Gouffier, was hot on the same trail. What the British Museum lost, the Louvre would gain. (One modern danger that Elgin could not have foreseen — and which alone suffices to justify his action — is the problem of chronic industrial air pollution. In the past years this scourge has seriously affected the fabric of all the Acropolis monuments.)

The Greek War of Independence, during which Byron met his melancholy death amid the lagoons of Missolonghi, heralded the last — and in a sense the strangest — period in the history of the Acropolis. The establishment of an autonomous kingdom in 1833, under an ardently philhellene Bavarian monarch, Otho I, at last turned Athena's rock over to the archaeologists, who in many ways dealt with it more savagely than even the Turks could have done. The demolition of Turkish and Frankish accretions began as early as 1833, and one of the first structures to disappear was the small mosque that had long stood inside the Parthenon itself — like a dirty cork in a beautiful bottle, as one scholar acidly described it. In 1834 Athens became the capital of liberated Greece, and a year later the Bavarian garrison left the Acropolis. Despite occasional protests, the destruction of all medieval and later buildings, the clearing of the Acropolis back to classical bedrock, went on apace. Between 1836 and 1842, the Athena Nike temple was reconstructed and work on the Erechtheum began. Major scientific excavations began around 1885 and were accompanied by

partial restoration of both the Erechtheum and Parthenon, work on the latter continuing until 1930. The area is still the subject of constant inspection and treatment.

Thus the Acropolis of Pericles and Athena Polias was once again exposed to view after two millennia of changing history. During that time classical Greece had, for long periods, been all but forgotten, and the eager tourists who crowd through the Beulé Gate today know little of the strange vicissitudes which that bare — and curiously bleak — rock has endured through the centuries. Yet they sense, rightly, that there once took place on that site an extraordinary flowering of the human spirit, an Icarus-like striving for glory and the sun. Although in ways this naked Acropolis has become unreal, an open-air museum, nevertheless those extraordinarily creative years in the fifth century B.C. still have the power to enthrall and quicken our understanding, generation by generation, today and for all time. "Not unwitnessed is our power," Pericles told his fellow citizens, "and we shall be the marvel of the present day and of ages yet to come." There can be few prouder boasts in history, and none that time has more triumphantly vindicated.

THE PARTHENON IN LITERATURE

Plutarch, the Greek biographer and moralist, came to Athens as a student in the mid-first century A.D. He died there some fifty years later, not long after the accession of Hadrian. His renowned Life of Pericles *contains a detailed account of the great temple-building program that took place on the Acropolis under Pericles's aegis. Although the temples themselves remained intact in Plutarch's time, the story of how they had come into being was no longer common knowledge. Their history needed to be told accurately and well, and Plutarch did precisely that, weaving a complex and highly charged portrait of Pericles into his description of the temples.*

That which gave most pleasure and ornament to the city of Athens, and the greatest admiration and even astonishment to all strangers, and that which now is Greece's only evidence that the power she boasts of and her ancient wealth are no romance or idle story, was his [Pericles's] construction of the public and sacred buildings. Yet this was that of all his actions in the government which his enemies most looked askance upon and cavilled at in the popular assemblies, crying out how that the commonwealth of Athens had lost its reputation and was ill-spoken of abroad for removing the common treasure of the Greeks from the isle of Delos into their own custody; and how that their fairest excuse for so doing, namely, that they took it away for fear the barbarians should seize it, and on purpose to secure it in a safe place, this Pericles had made unavailable, and how that "Greece cannot but resent it as an insufferable affront, and consider herself to be tyrannized over openly, when she sees the treasure, which was contributed by her upon a necessity for the war, wantonly lavished out by us upon our city, to gild her all over, and to adorn and set her forth, as it were some vain woman, hung round with precious stones and figures and temples, which cost a world of money."

Pericles, on the other hand, informed the people that they were in no way obliged to give any account of those moneys to their allies, so long as they maintained their defence, and kept off the barbarians from attacking them; while in the mean time they did not so much as supply one horse or man or ship, but only found money for the service; "which money," said he, "is not theirs that give it, but theirs that receive it, if so be they perform the conditions upon which they receive it." And that it was good reason, that, now the city was sufficiently provided and stored with all things necessary for the war, they should convert the overplus of its wealth to such undertakings, as would hereafter, when completed, give them eternal honor, and, for the present, while in process, freely supply all the inhabitants with plenty. With their variety of workmanship and of occasions for service, which summon all arts and trades and require all hands to be employed about them, they do actually put the whole city, in a manner, into state-pay; while at the same time she is both beautified and maintained by herself. For as those who are of age and strength for war are provided for and maintained in the armaments abroad by their pay out of the public stock, so, it being his desire and design that the undisciplined mechanic multitude that stayed at home should not go without their share of public salaries, and yet should not have them given them for sitting still and doing nothing, to that end he thought fit to bring in among them, with the approbation of the people, these vast projects of buildings and designs of works, that would be of some continuance before they were finished, and would give employment to

ATHENS'S FIRST HISTORIANS

The pencil sketch above, like those that illustrate pages 140–59, was executed by an anonymous Flemish draftsman who completed a critical series of studies of the Parthenon a few years before the structure's bombardment by the Venetians in 1687. His sketches, particularly those of the Parthenon frieze and pediments, have been of great value to students of Greek art.

numerous arts, so that the part of the people that stayed at home might, no less than those that were at sea or in garrisons or on expeditions, have a fair and just occasion of receiving the benefit and having their share of the public moneys.

The materials were stone, brass, ivory, gold, ebony cypress-wood; and the arts or trades that wrought and fashioned them were smiths and carpenters, moulders, founders and braziers, stone-cutters, dyers, goldsmiths, ivory-workers, painters, embroiderers, turners; those again that conveyed them to the town for use, merchants and mariners and ship-masters by sea, and by land, cartwrights, cattle-breeders, waggoners, rope-makers, flax-workers, shoe-makers and leather-dressers, road-makers, miners. And every trade in the same nature, as a captain in an army has his particular company of soldiers under him, had its own hired company of journeymen and laborers belonging to it banded together as in array, to be as it were the instrument and body for the performance of the service. Thus, to say all in a word, the occasions and services of these public works distributed plenty through every age and condition.

As then grew the works up, no less stately in size than exquisite in form, the workmen striving to outvie the material and the design with the beauty of their workmanship, yet the most wonderful thing of all was the rapidity of their execution. Undertakings, any one of which singly might have required, they thought, for their completion, several successions and ages of men, were every one of them accomplished in the height and prime of one man's political service. Although they say, too, that Zeuxis once, having heard Agatharchus the painter boast of despatching his work with speed and ease, replied, "I take a long time." For ease and speed in doing a thing do not give the work lasting solidity or exactness of beauty; the expenditure of time allowed to a man's pains beforehand for the production of a thing is repaid by way of interest with a vital force for its preservation when once produced. For which reason Pericles's works are especially admired, as having been made quickly, to last long. For every particular piece of his work was immediately, even at that time, for its beauty and elegance, antique; and yet in its vigor and freshness looks to this day as if it were just executed. There is a sort of bloom of newness upon those works of his, preserving them from the touch of time, as if they had some perennial spirit and undying vitality mingled in the composition of them.

Phidias had the oversight of all the works, and was surveyor-general, though upon the various portions other great masters and workmen were employed. For Callicrates and Ictinus built the Parthenon; the chapel at Eleusis, where the mysteries were celebrated, was begun by Coroebus, who erected the pillars that stand upon the floor or pavement, and joined them to the architraves; and after his death Metagenes of Xypete added the frieze and the upper line of columns; Xenocles of Cholargus roofed or arched the lantern on the top of the temple of Castor and Pollux; and the long wall, which Socrates says he himself heard Pericles propose to the people, was undertaken by Callicrates....

The Odeum, or music-room, which in its interior was full of seats and ranges of pillars, and outside had its roof made to slope and descend from one single point at the top, was constructed, we are told, in imitation of the king of Persia's Pavilion: this likewise by Pericles's order....

The propylaea, or entrances to the Acropolis, were finished in five years' time, Mnesicles being the principal architect. A strange accident happened in the course of building, which showed that the goddess was not averse to the work, but was aiding and coöperating to bring it to perfection. One of the artificers, the quickest and the handiest workman among them all, with a slip of his foot fell down from a great height, and lay in a miserable condition, the physicians having no hopes of his recovery. When Pericles was in distress about this, Minerva appeared to him at night in a dream, and ordered a course of treatment, which he applied, and in a short time and with great ease cured the man. And upon this occasion it was that he set up a brass statue of Minerva, surnamed Health, in the citadel near the altar, which they say was there before. But it was Phidias who wrought the goddess's image in gold, and he has his name inscribed on the pedestal as the workman of it; and indeed the whole work in a manner was under his charge, and he had, as we have said already, the oversight over all the artists and workmen, through Pericles's friendship for him; and this, indeed, made him much envied, and his patron shamefully slandered with stories, as if Phidias were in the habit of receiving, for Pericles's use, freeborn women that came to see the works. The comic writers of the town, when they had got hold of this story, made much of it, and bespattered him with all the ribaldry they could invent, charging him falsely with the wife of Menippus, one who was his friend and served as lieutenant under him in the wars; and with the birds kept by Pyrilampes, an acquaintance of Pericles, who, they pretended, used to give presents of peacocks to Pericles's female friends. And how can one wonder at any number of strange assertions from men whose whole lives were devoted to mockery, and who were ready at any time to sacrifice the reputation of their superiors to vulgar envy and spite, as to some evil genius, when even Stesimbrotus the Thasian has dared to lay to the charge of Pericles a monstrous and fabulous piece of criminality with his son's wife? So very difficult a matter is it to trace and find out the truth of any thing by history, when, on the one hand, those who afterwards write it find long periods of time intercepting their view, and, on the other hand, the contemporary records of any actions and lives, partly through envy and ill-will, partly through favor and flattery, pervert and distort truth.

PLUTARCH
Life of Pericles, c. A.D. 100

In the mid-second century A.D., *the travel writer Pausanias completed his rambling* Description of Greece, *a sporadically exhaustive and often carelessly researched overview of his native land. Despite its shortcomings, Pausanias's work is a trove of information on the architecture, sculpture, religion, and local traditions of ancient Greece. The excerpt which follows is based upon a visit that the author paid to the Parthenon shortly after Hadrian's restoration of both the Acropolis and the city of Athens itself.*

And as regards the temple which they call the Parthenon, as you enter it everything pourtrayed on the gables relates to the birth of Athene, and behind is depicted the contest between Poseidon and Athene for the soil of Attica. And this work of art is in ivory and gold. In the middle of her helmet is an image of the Sphinx — about whom I shall give an account when I come to Boeotia — and on each side of the helmet are griffins worked. These

griffins, says Aristus the Proconnesian in his poems, fought with the Arimaspians beyond the Issedones for the gold of the soil which the griffins guarded. And the Arimaspians were all one eyed men from their birth, and the griffins were beasts like lions, with wings and mouth like an eagle. Let so much suffice for these griffins. But the statue of Athene is full length, with a tunic reaching to her feet, and on her breast is the head of Medusa worked in ivory, and in one hand she has a Victory four cubits high, in the other hand a spear, and at her feet a shield, and near the spear a dragon which perhaps is Erichthonius. And on the base of the statue is a representation of the birth of Pandora, the first woman according to Hesiod and other poets, for before her there was no race of women. Here too I remember to have seen the only statue here of the Emperor Adrian, and at the entrance one of Iphicrates the celebrated Athenian general.

And outside the temple is a brazen Apollo said to be by Phidias: and they call it Apollo *Averter of Locusts,* because when the locusts destroyed the land the god said he would drive them out of the country. And they know that he did so, but they don't say how. I myself know of locusts having been thrice destroyed on Mount Sipylus, but not in the same way, for some were driven away by a violent wind that fell on them, and others by a strong blight that came on them after showers, and others were frozen to death by a sudden frost. All this came under my own notice.

PAUSANIAS
Description of Greece, c. A.D. 140

MINERVA'S TEMPLE

During the mid-seventeenth century, European antiquaries began arriving in Athens in small groups to examine the city's ancient monuments. Their timing was fortunate, for in 1687 a Venetian bomb exploded in the very heart of the Parthenon, shattering its millennium-old columns. As a result, we must depend upon the descriptions penned by these early visitors for most of what we know about key sculptures and decorations that were lost or heavily damaged in the explosion. One of the best of these accounts was written by George Wheler, an Englishman who visited Greece in the late 1670's with the celebrated classical antiquary, Jacob Spon. Minerva is, of course, the Roman equivalent of Athena.

We were so impatient to go to the Temple of *Minerva,* the chief Goddess of the *Athenians;* which is not only still the chief Ornament of the Cittadel; but absolutely, both for Matter and Art, the most beautiful piece of Antiquity remaining in the World. I wish, I could communicate the Pleasure I took in viewing it, by a Description, that would in some proportion express the *Ideas* I had then of it: which I cannot hope to do; but shall give you the Figure I took of it there, with its Dimensions, and so much of the Sculpture, as I can remember.

This Temple is called by *Pausanias, Parthenion;* because the Goddess *Minerva,* to whom it was dedicated, professed Virginity. It is situated about the middle of the Cittadel, and consists altogether of admirable white Marble. The Plane of it is above twice as long, as it is broad; being Two hundred, and seventeen foot, nine inches long, and ninety eight foot, six inches broad. It hath an Ascent, every way, of five Degrees, or Steps; which seem to be so contrived, to serve as a *Basis* to the *Portico;* which is supported by chanelled Pillars of the *Dorick* Order, erected round upon them, without any other *Basis*. These Pillars are Forty six in number, being eight to the Front, and as many behind, and seventeen on each side, counting the four corner ones twice over, to be deducted. They are Forty two foot high, and seventeen foot and a half about. The Distance between Pillar and Pillar, is seven foot, and four inches. This *Portico* beareth up a Front, and Frize round about the Temple, charged with Historical Figures of admirable Beauty and Work. The Figures of the Front, which the Ancients called the *Eagle*, appear, though from that height, of the natural bigness; being in entire *Relievo*, and wonderfully well carved. *Pausanias* saith no more of them, than that they concern the Birth of the Goddess *Minerva*. What I observed, and remember of them, is this.

There is a Figure, that stands in the middle of it, having its right Arm broken, which probably held the Thunder. Its Legs stradle at some distance from each other; where, without doubt, was placed the *Eagle:* For its Beard, and the Majesty, which the Sculpture hath expressed in his Countenance, although those other usual Characters be wanting here, do sufficiently show it to have been made for *Jupiter*. He stands naked; for so he was usually represented, especially by the *Greeks*. At his right hand is another Figure, with its Hands and Arms broken off, covered down half way the Leg, in a posture as coming towards *Jupiter;* which, perhaps, was a *Victory*, leading the Horses of the Triumphant Chariot of *Minerva*, which follows it. The Horses are made with such great Art, that the Sculptor seems to have out-done himself, by giving them a more than seeming Life: such a Vigour is express'd in each posture of their prauncing, and stamping, natural to generous Horses. *Minerva* is next represented in the Chariot, rather as the Goddess of *Learning*, than *War*, without Helmet, Buckler, or a *Medusa's* Head on her Breast, as *Pausanias* describes her Image within the Temple. Next behind her, is another Figure of a Woman sitting, with her Head broken off. Who it was, is not certain. But my Companion made me observe the next two Figures, sitting in the Corner, to be of the Emperour *Adrian*, and his Empress *Sabina;* whom I easily knew to be so, by the many Medals and Statues I have seen of them. . . .

. . . Within the *Portico* on high, and on the outside of the *Cella* of the Temple it self, is another Border of *Basso-relievo* round about it, or at least on the North and South-sides; which, without doubt, is as ancient as the Temple, and of admirable work; but not so high a *Relievo*, as the other. Thereon are represented Sacrifices, Processions, and other Ceremonies of the Heathens Worship. Most of them were designed by the Marquess *De Nantell;* who employed a Painter to do it two Months together, and shewed them to us, when we waited on him at *Constantinople*. The *Cella* of the Temple without, is a Hundred and fifty eight foot long, and broad Sixty seven foot. Before you enter into the Body of the Temple from the Front, is the *Pronaos*, whose Roof is sustained by six chanelled Pillars of the same order, and bigness with those of the *Portico*, and contains near the third part of the *Cella;* to wit, Forty four foot of the length. We observed in place of one of the Pillars, a great pile of Stone, and Lime, of most rude work; which they told us, the *Kizlar-Haga* had ordered to be so done, to help to support the Roof; because he could never find a Stone big enough to supply the place of the old Pillar, broken down; although he had spent Two thousand Crowns to do it. . . .

. . . There is also a great Vessel of white Marble, and curious Work, which

might have been a Font, to Baptize in, in time past: But not as Monsieur *Guiliter* affirmeth, for Holy-Water. For the *Greeks* use no such thing in their Churches, although they do at home, being made once a Year in the Church. Here hang also some few Lamps; that the *Turks* carry into the Temple, when they do their Night-Devotions. From the *Pronaos* we entred into the Temple, by a long Door in the middle of the Front. But my Companion, and I were not so much surprized with the Obscurity of it, as Monsieur *Guiliter;* because the Observations we had made on other Heathen Temples, did make it no new thing unto us, as I observed at *Spalato.* And that the Heathens loved Obscurity in their Religious Rites and Customs, many Reasons may be given; especially, because by that means the Pomps they exposed to the People, had much advantage by it; and the Defects of them, with all their juggling and cheating, were less exposed to view. When the *Christians* consecrated it to serve God in, they let in the Light at the East end; which is all that it yet hath. And not only that, but made a Semicircle for the Holy Place, according to their Rites; which the *Turks* have not yet much altered. This was separated from the rest by Jaspar Pillars; two of which, on each side, yet remain. Within this Chancel is a Canopy, sustained by four Porphyry Pillars, with beautiful white Marble Chapters, of the *Corinthian* Order. But the Holy Table under it, is removed. Beyond the Canopy are two or three Degrees, one above another, in a Semicircle; where the Bishops and Presbyters used to sit in time of Communion, upon certain Solemn days. The Bishop sate in a Marble Chair, above the rest; which yet remaineth above the Degrees, against the Window. Towards the bottom of this Window, are those marvelous Stones Monsieur *Guiliter* makes such a Miracle of. They are only of a transparent Marble; which *Pliny,* in the Thirtieth Book of his *Natural History,* calleth *Phengites;* and saith, It was found in *Capadocia,* in *Nero's* time, who built a Temple of it to Fortune; which was Light, when the Doors were shut. By reason of its Natural Transparency, an obscure Light passeth through it; and several Holes being made deep in it, it makes the Light look of a reddish, or yellowish colour. But as to its shining in the Night, that's a Wonder was never heard of until now; and for his comparing it to the Brightness of a Carbuncle, it may pass for one of his *Hyperbolies;* our Eyes being much too dim, to discover it. This same Author hath made many other Observations, whereof we could find but very little, or no probability; as the Inscription on this Temple, *To the unknown God,* the *Turks* Pilgrimages to it, with several others, not worth mentioning, and hardly to be excus'd from the Imputation of manifest Untruths. On both sides, and towards the Door, is a kind of Gallery, made with two Ranks of Pillars, Twenty two below, and Twenty three above. The odd Pillar is over the Arch of the Entrance, which was left for the Passage. It being now turn'd into a *Mosque,* the Niche of the *Turks Devotion* is made in the Corner on this side of the Altar, on the right hand; by which is their Place of Prayer: and on the other side a Pulpit, to read their Law in; as is usual in all *Mosques.* The *Turks,* according to their measure of Wit, have washed over the beautiful white Marble within, with Lime. At one side of the Quire, there are four Presses made in the Wall, and shut up with Doors of Marble. They say, None dares open them; and that one undertaking to do it, immediately died the first he opened; and that the Plague soon after followed in the Town. The Marquess of *Nantell* would have it attempted the second time; but the scrupulous *Turks* would not permit him. They think, there is some Treasure there; perhaps, there may be some Church-Vestments, Books, or Plate, belonging to the Altar; which now, in the poor *Greek* Church, is seldom much above a Chalice, and a small Silver Plate. They shewed us the place, where two Orange-trees of Marble had stood; which being taken thence to be carried to *Constantinople*, the Vessel miscarried with them. The Roof over the Altar and Quire, added to the Temple by the *Greeks*, hath the picture of the Holy Virgin on it, of *Mosaick* Work, left yet by the *Turks;* because, as they say, a certain *Turk* having shot a Musquet at it, his hand presently withered. This Temple was covered outwardly with great Planks of Stone; of which some are fallen down, and are to be seen in the *Mosque.* They have built a *Minoret,* or tall, slender Steeple; out of which they make a Noise, to call People together, at their set times of Prayer, day and night: On top of which I mounted, and had a most pleasing Prospect of the Cittadel, City, Plain, and Gulf of *Egina,* with the Coasts and Harbours round about. But I durst not stay long to enjoy the sight, for fear of being seen my self, and taken for one, that had other designs, than of meer Curiosity. After some small while therefore descending, we left the Temple of *Minerva;* having first made a Present of some few *Timins* to the *Turk,* who had been so civil to permit us such a free, and fair Examination of all the Mysteries, and Rarities of it.

GEORGE WHELER
A Journey into Greece, 1682

The Parthenon was sundered and most of its best statuary was pulverized on September 26, 1687, when a Venetian bomb detonated a powder magazine that had been hidden by the besieged Turks. At the time, the Parthenon also sheltered the governor's harem and a number of women and children, the Turks having assumed that the Christians would never bombard a former church. In the explosion, fragments of the Parthenon were scattered all over the Acropolis, and some three hundred deaths occurred as a result of the blast and ensuing fire. The event was described within the year by the Venetian Cristoforo Ivanovich, canon of St. Mark's Basilica.

His Excellency being informed that the Turks' ammunition was inside the Temple of Minerva along with their principal women and children, imagining themselves safe there because of the thickness of the walls and arches of the said temple, he ordered Count Mutoni to direct the firing of his bombs into that quarter. At first there arose some confusion in the trajectory of the bombs, which fell beyond the target. It was due to the inequality of weight which was of the order of 130 pounds variability from one bomb to another; but the correct charge being ascertained no longer overshot the mark; and thus, one of them hitting the flank of the temple ended by smashing it. The dreadful effect of this was a raging fury of fire and exploding powder and grenades, and the thundrous roar of the said ammunition discharging shook all the houses around, even in the suburbs outside the walls which were themselves a great city, and all this put fear in the hearts of the besieged. And thus was left in ruins that famous Temple of Minerva, which so many centuries and so many wars had not been able to destroy.

CRISTOFORO IVANOVICH
History of the Holy League Against the Turk, 1688

A MAGNIFICENT FABRIC

In 1763 the noted British antiquary Richard Chandler was commissioned to tour Greece and Asia Minor in the company of an architect and a painter and to study and record the fast-vanishing remains of Ionian civilization. The three published the results of their labors in two sumptuous folio volumes of Ionian antiquities, but Chandler also wrote a personal account of his travels, including his visit to the Athenian Acropolis in 1765.

The chief ornament of the acropolis was the parthenon or great temple of Minerva, a most superb and magnificent fabric. The Persians had burned the edifice, which before occupied the site, and was called hecatompedon, from its being an hundred feet square. The zeal of Pericles and of all the Athenians was exerted in providing a far more ample and glorious residence for their favourite goddess. The architects were Callicrates and Ictinus; and a treatise on the building was written by the latter and Carpion. It was of white marble, of the Doric order, the columns fluted and without bases, the number in front eight; and adorned with admirable sculpture. The story of the birth of Minerva was carved in the front pediment; and in the back, her contest with Neptune for the country. The beasts of burthen, which had conveyed up the materials, were regarded as sacred, and recompensed with pastures; and one, which had voluntarily headed the train, was maintained during life, without labour, at the public expense.

The statue of Minerva, made for this temple by Phidias, was of ivory, twenty six cubits or thirty nine feet high. It was decked with pure gold to the amount of forty four talents, so disposed by the advice of Pericles as to be taken off and weighed, if required. The goddess was represented standing, with her vestment reaching to her feet. Her helmet had a Sphinx for the crest, and on the sides were Griffins. The head of Medusa was on her breast-plate. In one hand she held her spear, and in the other supported an image of Victory about four cubits high. . . . This image was placed in the temple in the first year of the eighty-seventh Olympiad, in which the Peloponnesian war began. The gold was stripped off by the tyrant Lachares, when Demetrius Poliorcetes compelled him to fly. The same plunderer plucked down the golden shields in the acropolis, and carried away the golden Victories, with the precious vessels and ornaments provided for the Panathenaean festival. . . .

The parthenon remained entire for many ages after it was deprived of the goddess. The Christians converted it into a church, and the Mahometans into a mosque. It is mentioned in the letters of Crusius, and miscalled the *pantheon*, and the temple of *the unknown god*. The Venetians under Koningsmark, when they besieged the acropolis in 1687, threw a bomb, which demolished the roof, and, setting fire to some powder, did much damage to the fabric. The floor, which is indented, still witnesses the place of its fall. This was the sad forerunner of farther destruction, the Turks breaking the stones, and applying them to the building of a new mosque, which stands within the ruin, or to the repairing of their houses and the walls of the fortress. The vast pile of ponderous materials, which lay ready, is greatly diminished; and the whole structure will gradually be consumed and disappear. . . .

It is not easy to conceive a more striking object than the parthenon, though now a mere ruin. The columns within the naos have all been removed, but on the floor may be seen the circles, which directed the workmen in placing them; and at the farther end is a groove across it, as for one of the partitions of the cell. The recess erected by the Christians is demolished, and from the rubbish of the ceiling the Turkish boys collect bits of the Mosaic, of different colours, which composed the picture. We were told at Smyrna, that this substance had taken a polish, and been set in buckles. The cell is about half demolished, and in the columns, which surrounded it, is a large gap near the middle. On the walls are some traces of the painting. Before the portico is a reservoir, sunk in the rock, to supply the Turks with water for the purifications customary on entering their mosques. In it on the left hand is the rubbish of the pile erected to supply the place of a column; and on the right, a staircase which leads out on the architrave, and has a marble or two with inscriptions, but worn so as not to be legible. It belonged to the minaret, which has been destroyed.

RICHARD CHANDLER
Travels in Greece, 1776

Edward Dodwell, English traveler, collector of antiquities, and writer on archaeology, left England when he was in his early thirties and spent most of the remainder of his life in Italy. From 1801 to 1806, Dodwell traveled in Greece. Visiting Athens in 1806, he devoted days to the Acropolis, studying the monuments and sketching them with the aid of a portable camera obscura. Prototype of the modern camera, the camera obscura had been in fairly common use as a sketching instrument throughout the eighteenth century, but Dodwell's may have been the first ever seen in Athens. Its appearance on the Acropolis led to an interesting confrontation with the Turkish governor.

The Acropolis first attracts the curiosity of the traveller, and merits as much attention as all the lower town; for what is there in Athens that can compare with the Acropolis in antiquity, in splendour, or in interest? Upon a first admission within these venerable walls, it is necessary to make a small present to the Disdar, or Turkish governor; and an additional present is required for permission at any future time to make drawings and observations, without being molested by the soldiers of the garrison. The whole of these presents generally amount to eighty or a hundred Turkish piastres.

Being aware, from the experience I had had on my former visit to Athens, that the Disdar was a man of bad faith and insatiable rapacity, I made him a small present the first day, and begged the English agent to conclude a bargain with him for eighty piastres; in consideration of which, I was to have free access to the Acropolis as often as I chose. In order to prevent the Disdar from exacting a larger sum, it was stipulated that the payment should take place after I had completed all my drawings and observations. Many days however had not elapsed before the Disdar became impatient for the money, and asked me for a part of the promised sum: upon my refusal of which he prohibited my admission to the Acropolis. But when I returned, I succeeded in gaining an entrance, after enduring some insolent speeches from the soldiers, which I pretended not to understand. At length however I obtained their good graces by making some small presents to their children, who became so accustomed to this kind of tribute, that they used to watch for me over the wall of the citadel; and whenever I returned I always found them collected at the door. By throwing a few paras amongst them, I acquired the name of the Frank of many Paras, and for a small expense purchased the civility of the soldiers. The Disdar, however, became more and more im-

patient for the promised present; and in order to save time, I frequently sent my dinner up to the Acropolis; and with my artist, employed the whole day in drawing. The Disdar watched the arrival of the dinner as eagerly as the children did the distribution of the paras, and seldom failed to drink the greater part of our wine; observing, that wine was not good for studious people like us.

After experiencing numerous vexations from this mercenary Turk, a ridiculous circumstance at length released us from the continuance of his importunities. I was one day engaged in drawing the Parthenon with the aid of my camera obscura, when the Disdar, whose surprise was excited by the novelty of the sight, asked with a sort of fretful inquietude, what new conjuration I was performing with that extraordinary machine? I endeavoured to explain it, by putting in a clean sheet of paper, and making him look into the camera obscura; he no sooner saw the temple instantaneously reflected on the paper in all its lines and colours, than he imagined that I had produced the effect by some magical process; his astonishment appeared mingled with alarm, and stroking his long black beard, he repeated the words *Allah, Masch-Allah*, several times. He again looked into the camera obscura with a kind of cautious diffidence, and at that moment some of his soldiers happening to pass before the reflecting glass, were beheld by the astonished Disdar walking upon the paper: he now became outrageous; and after calling me pig, devil, and Buonoparte, he told me, that if I chose, I might take away the temple and all the stones in the citadel; but that he would never permit me to conjure his soldiers into my box. When I found that it was in vain to reason with his ignorance, I changed my tone, and told him that if he did not leave me unmolested, I would put *him* into my box; and that he should find it a very difficult matter to get out again. His alarm was now visible; he immediately retired, and ever after stared at me with a mixture of apprehension and amazement. When he saw me come to the Acropolis, he carefully avoided my approach; and never afterwards gave me any further molestation.

It is a humiliating reflection that such extreme ignorance should be found within the precincts of a temple, where the Goddess of Wisdom was once not only worshipped by the populace, but received the homage even of the wise.

EDWARD DODWELL
A Classical and Topographical Tour Through Greece, 1806

PILGRIMAGE OF A ROMANTIC

Lord Byron was twenty-two when he paid his first visit to Athens, arriving on Christmas Day, 1809. He tarried ten weeks, working on Childe Harold's Pilgrimage, *the epic poem that was to bring him instant fame upon its publication three years later. Byron's traveling companion was John Cam Hobhouse, an impassioned admirer of ancient monuments who used the occasion to alert fellow romantics in Europe to the fact that the temples on the Acropolis were deteriorating rapidly and would soon be gone unless something was done in the very near future to save them.*

The portion of the Parthenon yet standing, cannot fail to fill the mind of the most indifferent spectator with sentiments of astonishment and awe, and the same reflections arise upon the sight even of the enormous masses of marble ruins which are spread upon the area of the Temple. Such scattered fragments will soon constitute the sole remains of the Temple of Minerva.

If the progress of decay should continue to be as rapid as it has been for something more than a century past, there will, in a few years, be not one marble standing upon another on the site of the Parthenon. In 1667, every antiquity of which there is now any trace in the Acropolis, was in a tolerable state of preservation. This great Temple might, at that period, be called entire — having been previously a Christian church, it was then a mosck, the most beautiful in the world. At present, only twenty-nine of the Doric columns, some of which no longer support their entablatures, and part of the left wall of the cell, remain standing. Those of the north side, the angular ones excepted, have all fallen: the dipteral porches, especially the Pronaos, contain the greatest number. . . .

In the interval between two of my visits to the Acropolis. . . . The figure of Victory . . . has been recovered by Lord Elgin's agents, who demolished a Turkish house close to the north-west angle of the Temple, for the purposes of excavation, and found it, as well as small parts of the Jupiter, the Vulcan, and the Minerva, underneath the modern building, where they had lain since the Venetians had unsuccessfully attempted to remove them in 1687. (The ropes by which . . . the workmen were lowering them, broke, and many fine figures were dashed to pieces. Lord Elgin has reaped the advantage of the sacrilege of the Venetians.) . . .

Within the cell of the Temple all is desolation and ruin; the shafts of columns, fragments of the entablatures, and of the beams of the roof, are scattered about on every side, but especially on the north of the area, where there are vast piles of marble. I measured one piece, seventeen feet in length, and of proportionate breadth and thickness. The floor, also of marble, has been broken up towards the eastern front, and in the southeast angle of the area, is the wretched mosck, as well as some stone-work of the Greek church, into which the Parthenon was formerly converted. A dent in the floor is pointed out as being occasioned by the shell which blew up in a powder-magazine, and destroyed the roof of the Temple, when bombarded by Morosini. . . .

The part of the area the most clear from ruins, is towards the north-west angle, and the western entrance, where the grooves in the floor, formed by opening and shutting the folding-doors of the Temple, are still very discernible. Faint marks of the painted saints, with which the Christians disfigured the interior of their Pagan edifice, are just visible on the walls of the south side of the cell. . . .

Descending from the ruins of the Parthenon to the north, you pass through a lane or two of white-washed cottages in ruins, before you come to the remains of the Erecthéum, and the adjoining chapel of Pandrosos. In that portion of the Erecthéum which was dedicated to Minerva Polias, the columns of the front porch are standing, but without any part of their entablature, and unsupported by the walls of the cell, the whole of the south side of which was destroyed during the short war between England and Turkey, and now lies in heaps at the back of the columns, and in the area of the Temple. The corner one of these columns, the best specimen of the Ionic in the world, with its base and capital, has been removed by Lord Elgin to England. The remainder will soon fall.

JOHN CAM HOBHOUSE
A Journey Through Albania and Other Provinces of Turkey in Europe and Asia to Constantinople, 1813

THE ACROPOLIS BESIEGED

Since Mycenaean times, the Acropolis has been besieged again and again. The capitulation of 1822, in which Turkish defenders surrendered to Greek insurgents after a protracted siege, was described some years later by an American named Samuel Gridley Howe, who spent six years as a soldier and surgeon in the Greek army during that country's war for independence. Returning to America, Howe married Julia Ward, who later composed The Battle Hymn of the Republic, *and together they edited* The Commonwealth, *an important voice in the antislavery movement. Samuel Howe epitomized nineteenth-century democratic idealism, and it is fitting that the opening chapter of his career should have been devoted to the cause of Greek independence.*

At the commencement of the revolt, the inhabitants of Athens retired to Salamis, and left the Turks in quiet possession of the Acropolis; . . . in a few months they issued from Salamis, and commenced the blockade of the Acropolis. That blockade was continued for some time, and the Turks began to feel the effects of famine; when the advance of Omer Pashaw, relieved the place, and drove the Greeks again to take refuge in Salamis. Omer, while he remained in Athens, was guilty of the greatest enormities to those of the Greeks who were unfortunate enough to fall into his hands. He ravaged Attica, burnt the villages, and destroyed the crops. . . .

But Omer soon retired from Athens, leaving it well garrisoned. Hardly had he gone, when the Athenians, issuing again from Salamis, obliged the Turks to evacuate the lower town of Athens, and shut themselves up in the Acropolis; the blockade of which was immediately recommenced.

This had now been continued several months, and the very remarkable fact of no rain having fallen to fill the cisterns of the Acropolis, reduced the Turks to the greatest distress. The Greeks had made an assault, intended to carry the citadel; they had failed in this object, but got possession of the spring just without the walls, which had heretofore supplied the Turks with water. They also had brought a few miserable cannon, and a pair of mortars, with which they cannonaded and bombarded the fortress; but this had but little effect upon the garrison, who were suffering however from thirst. During the siege, proof was given of that affection which Mussulmen have for animals, and which seems more remarkable when contrasted with their cruelties to men. They were seen to lower down their mules, jackasses, dogs, and cats, from the precipitous sides of the Acropolis, and let them fall into the hands of their enemies, rather than kill them, or let them die of thirst in the citadel. Nay, several mules were preserved alive to the very end of the siege by their masters, who had probably some secret supply of water, while many of their fellow-men had perished from thirst.

The Greeks continued to press the siege in their rude way, with their rude materials, notwithstanding they made so little impression. But it was necessary to do something, and the whims of several fanfaronading European officers, who were continually talking about approaches and contrevallations, and blinds and gabions, must be complied with: so the siege, as it was called, went on.

But no rain fell in the Acropolis; the rainy season was passing away; the surrounding country was deluged with showers; the olive-groves were blooming in their verdure, which the rain continually brightened; and the besieged saw the heavens covered with clouds every where, except just over their heads; they divided and passed by the Acropolis on each side, and showered their contents upon the plains: while the Turks, parched with thirst on the dry top of the Acropolis, called in vain on Allah to send them one single shower. But none came; the rainy season passed entirely away; the bright transparent sky of Attica was again without a cloud, without a single speck for the eye to rest upon. Had Allah deserted them? The Turks thought so; and after suffering from thirst for many days, during which they every night licked off with their tongues the moisture that gathered on the columns and marbles of the Parthenon and other buildings, they at last capitulated to the Greeks on the 21st.

The garrison, eleven hundred in number, gave up their arms, and stipulated only for their lives, and a small quantity of baggage for each person, with which they were to be transported to Asia Minor. But even these hard terms were not observed, for the very next day some of the Turks were put to death. This, however, was but what in the East would be considered fair retaliation for a previous outrage of the Turks. When the insurrection first broke out in the north, and long before it reached Attica, the Turks had taken ten Athenians, heads of families, by force, and kept them in the Acropolis as hostages. Soon after, when the Athenians rose, they took about fifty Turks prisoners, and in order to insure them their lives, they delivered them to the Austrian Consul for safe keeping. In a day or two after, the Turks being besieged in the Acropolis, amused themselves with killing their Greek hostages, and hanging their bodies over the wall. The friends of these murdered men swore vengeance. And the day after the capitulation, they in some way obtained possession of the persons of ten Turks, took them to the very spot where their own friends had been butchered, and there put them to death, in atonement for the blood of the ten hostages.

SAMUEL GRIDLEY HOWE
An Historical Sketch of the Greek Revolution, 1828

MELVILLE'S ALTERED VISION

In October 1856, Herman Melville sailed from New York on an eight-month cruise that was to take him to Egypt, Palestine, Italy, and Greece. Moby Dick was a half-dozen years behind him, and his mood was one of intense disillusionment and despair. He had come to a turning point in his life, and he felt that he needed a change of scenery. But as his intimate friend Nathaniel Hawthorne noted at the time, Melville "did not anticipate much pleasure in his rambles, for that spirit of adventure is gone out of him." In this frame of mind, Melville produced a bleak record of his visit to the Parthenon, recorded in idiosyncratic fashion in his personal journal.

F*eb 8th Sunday . . . Acropolis* — blocks of marble like . . . huge cakes of wax. — Parthenon elevated like cross of Constantine. Strange contrast of rugged rock with polished temple. . . . Imperceptible seams — frozen together. — Break like cakes of snow. . . .
Feb 10th Among the ruins — revisited them all. . . . Pavement of Parthenon — square — blocks of ice. (frozen together.) — No morter: — Delicacy of frostwork. . . .
Feb 11th Wednesday. Clear & beautiful day. Fine ride on box to Pireus. Acropolis in sight nearly whole way. Straight road. . . . Pentelicus covered at top with snow — looking down on its child, the Parthenon. — Ruins of Parthenon like North River breaking up.

Upon his return to America, Melville began to experiment with poetry, and a number of those early verses evoke the places that the American novelist had visited on his Mediterranean tour. In one of them, The Parthenon, *he paints a verbal picture that is markedly different from the one recorded in his journal. Seen from afar and in its original glory, the great temple is "a suncloud motionless in noon of day divine."*

I.
Seen aloft from afar.

ESTRANGED in site,
Aerial gleaming, warmly white,
You look a suncloud motionless
In noon of day divine;
Your beauty charmed enhancement takes
In Art's long after-shine.

II.
Nearer viewed.

Like Lais, fairest of her kind,
In subtlety your form's defined —
The cornice curved, each shaft inclined,
While yet, to eyes that do but revel
   And take the sweeping view,
Erect this seems, and that a level,
   To line and plummet true.

Spinoza gazes; and in mind
Dreams that one architect designed
   Lais — and you!

III.
The Frieze.

What happy musings genial went
With airiest touch the chisel lent
   To frisk and curvet light
Of horses gay — their riders grave —
Contrasting so in action brave
   With virgins meekly bright,
Clear filing on in even tone
With pitcher each, one after one
   Like water-fowl in flight.

IV.
The Last Tile.

When the last marble tile was laid
The winds died down on all the seas;
   Hushed were the birds, and swooned the glade;
   Ictinus sat; Aspasia said
"Hist! — Art's meridian, Pericles!"

HERMAN MELVILLE
The Parthenon, c. 1860

The publication in 1863 of La Vie de Jésus *by the French philosopher and historian Ernest Renan touched off an international furor. The very notion of a biography of Jesus was considered blasphemous by most of the Christians who read the book — and many did as the scandal spread and* The Life of Jesus *was translated into one language after another. Meanwhile, Renan himself left Europe for the Middle East. The year 1865 found him in Athens, where his intensely emotional reaction to the Parthenon resulted in* Prayer on the Acropolis, *a confession of faith in pure reason and art. Renan's little pamphlet, which modern readers find extravagantly overwritten, was carried reverently to Athens by a generation of like-minded pilgrims.*

O noble! O simple and true beauty! Goddess whose creed signifies reason and wisdom, thou whose temple is an eternal lesson of conscience and sincerity, I have arrived late at the threshold of thy mysteries. I bring to thy altar a deep remorse. . . . The initiation, bestowed by thee on the infant Athenian with a smile, I have conquered by force of reflection and at the price of a long struggle.

Goddess of the azure eyes, I was born of parents who were barbarians, in the domain of the good and virtuous Cimmerians who dwell on the rockbound shore of a somber sea, ever assailed by storms. . . .

My ancestors, as far as I can remember back, were mariners who sailed, on distant quests, seas unknown to the Argonauts. I heard them tell, when I was a child, of hyperborean voyages. My cradle memories teem with sifting snow, with wintry seas the hue of milk, with isles peopled by countless birds, which, taking flight together, obscured the sky.

SIMPLE AND TRUE BEAUTY

152

Priests of a strange religion, having its origin among the Syrians of Palestine, made it their duty to instruct me. They were wise and holy men. They acquainted me with the long chronicle of Kronos, the deity who created the world, and whose son, they averred, had lived as a man upon the earth. Their temples are thrice as high as thine . . . with roofs that tower like forests; but they are without solidity, and crumble to ruin at the end of five or six centuries. They are the follies of barbarians who imagine they can erect something substantial which is not in accordance with the rules thou hast given to thy inspired ones, O Reason! . . .

The world will never be saved unless it returns to thee, and repudiates its barbaric attachments. Let us run to thee, let us come in a great throng! What a day of splendor that will be when all the cities that have taken from the wreck of thy temple, making reparation for their larcenies, form a sacred procession to carry back the marbles they possess, and say to thee; "Pardon us, Goddess, it was only to save them from the evil genii of the night!" And they will rebuild thy walls to the sound of the flute. . . . I would rather be the last in thy house than the first elsewhere. Yes, I will attach myself to the stylobate of thy temple. I will forget all discipline except thine. I will make me a stylite on thy columns, my cell will be on thy architrave. Something more difficult! For thee, I will become intolerant, prejudiced. I will adore none but thee. I will try at once to learn thy language, to forget all the rest. I will be unjust to those that come not near thee. I will make myself the servant of the last of thy devotees. Those who now inhabit the land that thou gavest to Erechtheus, I will exalt them, I will flatter them. I will strive to love them for their faults. I will persuade myself, O Hippia, that they are the descendants of the cavaliers who celebrate, aloft on thy marble frieze, their eternal holiday. I will tear from my heart every fibre which is not reason and pure art. . . .

Thou art true, pure, perfect! Thy marble has no stain. But the temple of Hagia-Sophia, at Byzantium, yields, too, a divine effect with its brick and plaster. It is built to resemble the vault of heaven. It will crumble. But if thy sanctuary was large enough to contain a vast throng, it would crumble also.

An immense wave of oblivion sweeps us to a nameless abyss. O Abyss, thou art the only God! The tears of all men are true tears, the visions of all the wise contain a gleam of truth. Everything here below is but symbol and dream. Gods pass as men, and it is well that they should not be immortal. Faith that one has had should never be a chain. We lay it aside when we roll it carefully in the purple shroud where sleep the dead Gods.

ERNEST RENAN
Prayer on the Acropolis, 1865

The first modern Olympic Games were held in Athens in the spring of 1896. American athletes won nine of the twelve track and field events and two of the five shooting events. Along with the Greek winner of the marathon, they were the heroes of the hour. Another young American in Athens won glory of a different sort earlier that same year by solving the riddle of the nail holes in the east front of the Parthenon. Archaeologists had long known that the nails once secured metal letters that spelled out an inscription, but it was impossible to analyze the pattern without getting close to it — at a height of forty-five feet from the ground. High winds over the Acropolis and the instability of parts of the Parthenon itself made the task even more dangerous. One volunteer, Eugene P. Andrews, was a student at the American Classical School in Athens.

THE RIDDLE OF THE EAST FRIEZE

One cold afternoon in December a group of shivering men and women followed a lecturer in and out among the blocks of marble that strew the Acropolis of Athens, and listened as he explained the problems which the great building before them presents. It was an illustrated lecture on the Parthenon, with the Parthenon itself for illustration — one of the outdoor archaeological lectures which Dr. Wilhelm Dörpfeld of the German Institute gives every Saturday afternoon during the winter. The lectures are primarily for the men of the institute, but members of the other archaeological schools receive a kindly welcome; and Englishmen, Italians, Americans, and Greeks avail themselves gladly of the opportunity to wander through the ancient city with such a guide. Boreas was asserting his sway in his own dominion in vigorous fashion that week. As his ulster-clad victims tried to keep out of the reach of the cutting blasts that swept the bleak waste of rock, and as the hum of the city, bearing a street-cry here and there, swirled up to them with the dust-clouds from the plain, the legend of Oreithyia, the maiden snatched away by the North Wind from the hillside across the valley, suddenly took new meaning, and the rise of such a story was easy to understand. It was my good fortune to be a member of the American school, and therefore one of the audience. We were gathered before the east front of the temple. With heads tilted back and aching necks, we followed the lecturer where his words were leading us, while the problems of column, architrave, triglyph, and the rest were made so plain that we forgot the ache, and wondered why we had never understood it all before. Learned men have written great books about the building that rose before us; mighty battles of logic or opinion have been fought over almost every detail; each of its marble blocks has been measured with a painstaking accuracy that would be ridiculous were it any other building than the Parthenon: but "all the Old World's culture culminated in Greece, all Greece in Athens, all Athens in its Acropolis, all the Acropolis in the Parthenon." Racked by earthquake and torn by explosion, bombarded and pillaged by Christian and Turk, for centuries a rich mine for lime-burner and museum-pirate, its fair white brow turned golden brown with the suns and winds and driving rains of more than two thousand years, it yet stands peerless in all the world. Our architects have not caught up with those old pagans who built this temple for their virgin goddess twenty-three hundred years ago. They are still imitating it, and trying to master the principles of its construction and the art of the man who planned it. Again and again it has been covered with elaborate and expensive scaffolding, that no detail be missed. We were unprepared, therefore, to learn that anything remained to be found out about the building; a riddle was the last thing that we expected. Our attention was directed once more, however, to the architrave, normally a smooth surface of marble, an unbroken band of brown, a hundred feet long and four feet wide, running across the whole front just above the tops of the eight columns. It is the surface of the great marble beams which span from pillar to pillar. Above it runs a belt of about the same width composed of fifteen three-barred triglyphs alternating with fourteen sculptured metopes. There is a triglyph over each column, and one in the middle of each of the intervening spaces. Under each metope there is a hole, four inches by two, cut in the marble of the architrave, and under each of twelve of the triglyphs is a close group of smaller holes arranged with no apparent system.

"The large holes," explained the lecturer, "once served to hold great metal shields in place against the marble. The weathering about the holes shows that the shields were approximately four feet in diameter, and the contrast with the weathering outside the four-foot circle shows that they remained some time in place. Between the shields groups of metal letters were fastened, as these nail-holes that dot the spaces show, but what the letters were, or what they spelled, is not known. It is, without doubt, possible to determine from the relative positions of the holes what the letters were, and thus to recover the inscription. Such things have been done, and it is time that this were done."

The suggestion was inspiring, and as soon as possible permission to undertake the work was obtained from Mr. Kabbadias, General Ephor of Antiquities. . . .

. . . During their occupation the Turks made the Parthenon a mosque and built a minaret in its southwest corner. The top of the minaret, which was once a prominent feature of all views of the Acropolis, disappeared long ago; but its spiral stairway is still in place, and renders ascent to the top of the west end an easy matter. The east front, however, stands alone, and has escaped the visits of the man who scratches his pitiful name on the homes of the gods; for its top is inaccessible, except by means of ladders, scaffolding, or ropes. All attempts, therefore, to obtain an accurate transcription of the holes have been made from below, with the aid of opera-glasses or long-range cameras. The height, forty-five feet, and the fact that at such a distance spots of Turkish bullet-marks are not easily to be distinguished from nail-holes, have combined to make these attempts uniformly unsuccessful, and direct access to the architrave seemed to be not only desirable, but necessary.

The use of ladders was out of the question. All building in Greece is done from scaffolds the levels of which are connected by inclined planes of boards, and there is probably not a ladder fifty feet long in all the kingdom. A scaffold seemed too cumbrous and expensive to be considered as a possibility. It was necessary, therefore, to get a rope over the top. A stone with a string attached was thrown over, stronger cords were drawn after it, and at last a stout Manila rope was dragged across the cornice, and lay with one end hanging down in the portico and the other dropping to the steps outside. A pulley was tied to the latter end, and as the rope was hauled back over the cornice the pulley mounted to the edge, carrying up with it a rope which had been reeved through it. The pulley was held firmly aloft by making the end of the rope that supported it fast around the foot of one of the columns. Sitting in a swing attached to one end of the rope that ran through the pulley, I could pull down on the other end, and thus raise myself to the architrave and get within reach of the puzzle.

A glance along the great surface of battered marble showed that it would be necessary to make some sort of cast of the different groups of holes, so that the inscription might be studied in its entirety and a comparative method followed. The use of squeeze-paper suggested itself. This is a wood-pulp paper which is used to take impressions, known technically as "squeezes," of inscriptions cut in stone — a paper that is plastic when wet and stiff when dry. From the ground each group of holes is strikingly like the top of a pepper-box in appearance; but when one swings before them, it is seen that the holes are well cut, as a rule three quarters of an inch long by half an inch wide, over half an inch deep, and from two to three inches apart. A sheet of paper was spread over the stone, wet with a sponge, and pounded tight to the surface with a brush. It broke through wherever it stretched across a hole. Two strips of paper, wet and crossing each other at right angles, were pushed in by their middle through each break to the bottom of the hole, so that each hole was lined with a double U of paper. The four projecting ends of the strips were turned back flat on the paper, and another sheet was put against the first. Both sheets were next thoroughly wet and pounded into a coherent mass of pulp, and the ends of the strips were thus held firmly between. If the wind did not blow the squeeze down during the night, it was stiff and strong in the morning; a little careful use of a paper-knife pried the knobs out of the holes; and a cast was secured which showed with entire accuracy the relative position of the holes, their shape, depth, and direction. It took all day to make a cast of one group of holes, and there are twelve groups. At that season of the year the chances were that a wind would rise during the night, and that I should find the great sheet of paper, torn and rumpled, snugly wedged among the blocks of marble about the corner on the south side of the Parthenon. As a rule, two could be secured in a week and carried safely to the school, a mile away. Any one who knows anything of the Greek temperament can imagine that the sight of the great white paper covered with knobs and flapping like a sail in the wind — for of course it could not be rolled — never failed to arouse the most active interest in its procession through the busy street of Aeolus, up Hermes street, and across the promenade before the palace. After a month and a half the great pile of knobby papers in the library of the school was complete, and it ceased to be my first care in the morning to examine the east architrave of the Parthenon with a field-glass from a window of my room, to see if the squeeze had survived the night.

The work, without doubt, owes its completion to Dr. Dörpfeld's kindness, which made it possible to substitute a strong rope-ladder belonging to the German school for the swing at the end of a rope running through a pulley. This ladder was long enough to reach to the top of the building, and it was thus possible to determine from which of the projecting blocks it would be unwise to suspend any weight. Two were found to be badly broken, but fortunately the string which was thrown over at first had fallen on a block that is firm. The swing was now hung from the ladder, and by climbing to the top and lifting the ladder along, it was comparatively easy to gain access to any part of the architrave. The rope at the upper end of the ladder crossed over the top of the cornice, dropped down on the inside, and was made fast around the foot of the nearest column, just as had been done with the rope from the pulley. When the use of the pulley was discontinued, after only two impressions had been obtained, the rope which held it aloft was found to be cut half through by the edge of marble over which it had hung. The access which the ladder gave to the top made it possible to protect the ropes from similar cutting by wrapping them carefully with cloth.

The paper casts were hung in order about a room in the school, and thus the inscription could be studied with greater convenience than even from a scaffold running the whole length of the architrave. It has been generally assumed that the letters spelled the clever message that Alexander the Great sent to Athens, only a hundred years after the Parthenon was completed, with the three hundred suits of armor from the booty of his first Asiatic victory at the Granikos:

ALEXANDER, SON OF PHILIP, AND
THE GREEKS, EXCEPT THE LACEDAEMONIANS,
FROM THE BARBARIANS
WHO INHABIT ASIA.

The suits of armor were sent to be placed in the Acropolis in honor of Athena, and the message was to be erected with them as a dedicatory inscription. What more natural than that the Athenians, gratified that Alexander, even if he was a Macedonian and their own conqueror, should desire to have it appear that he had undertaken the conquest of Persia in the name of Greece; and in the name of all Greece, except hated Sparta, should hang the shields in exultation on Athena's very temple, and write between them the words which proclaimed them the first-fruits of revenge on the grandsons of the Persian invaders? The most casual review of the nail-holes, however, was enough to convince one that this could not have been the Alexander message; for, while that contains in Greek only ninety-four letters, the Parthenon inscription had evidently contained not less than two hundred and fifty letters, arranged in three lines.

The Parisian makers of the great model of the Parthenon in the Metropolitan Museum of Art in New York evidently recognized this difficulty. When they attempted to reproduce the inscription between the shields on the east front, they found that the Alexander message would fill only about one third of the spaces. (It should be observed that they assumed thirteen groups of letters instead of twelve.) They considered themselves obliged, therefore, to introduce matter of their own invention, reference to other victories of Alexander for the most part, sufficient to bring the number of letters up to three hundred and thirty-five.

But to return to Athens. There was little time wasted in guessing. Groups of holes which were repeated here and there were picked out, measured accurately, and classified. In a short time there were almost as many of these different combinations as there are letters in the Greek alphabet. . . .

Identification of the letters from the patterns made by the nail holes was a difficult and fascinating puzzle. Andrews gives a detailed account of it. The emerging reconstructed inscription turned out to be in honor of Nero, and not Alexander's Persian conquest. The story continues:

More than half yet remains to be read, but with so many letters identified and at our command, the deciphering goes fast, and the rest is soon legible. . . . The formula is complete, and it is evident that the inscription commemorated the erection of a statue of Nero, probably at the entrance of the Parthenon:

> THE COUNCIL OF THE AREIOPAGOS AND THE COUNCIL OF
> THE SIX HUNDRED AND THE ATHENIAN PEOPLE [ERECT A
> STATUE OF] EMPEROR GREATEST NERO CAESAR CLAUDIUS
> AUGUSTUS GERMANICUS, SON OF GOD, WHILE TI[BERIUS]
> CLAUDIUS NOVIUS SON OF PHILINOS IS ACTING AS GENERAL
> OVER THE HOPLITES FOR THE EIGHTH TIME, AND WHILE
> HE IS OVERSEER AND LAWGIVER.

This Novius is prominent in the history of his time, and held several offices besides those enumerated; but he seems to have thought that it would be unwise to occupy more than half of the inscription with his own titles, even if they were used ostensibly to date the event. Neither the eighth year of his generalship nor the name of the priestess for the year, which is given, but has not yet been deciphered, would avail to date the inscription accurately, were it not for the fact that there is in existence another inscription which not only states that Novius was general for the eighth time, but deigns to give the name of the archon — Thrasyllos — who was in office that year. Phlegon, in one of his "Wonder Stories," tells of a four-headed child that was brought to Nero in the archonship of Thrasyllos, while Caesonius Paetus and Petronius Turpilianus were consuls in Rome. The year of their consulship was 61 A.D., and this chain of references locates the Parthenon inscription in the same year.

EUGENE P. ANDREWS
"How a Riddle of the Parthenon Was Unraveled," 1896

The Parthenon never had a more enthusiastic visitor than Isadora Duncan. Her first pilgrimage to the sacred mount occurred late in 1903 and culminated in a family recitation of Renan's Prayer on the Acropolis, *led by the twenty-five-year-old Isadora. For the next four months, the young dancer haunted the Parthenon — until at last she received a revelation pertaining to her future as an artist.*

SPIRIT AND FORM

Anyone who, arriving at the foot of the Acropolis, has mounted with prayerful feet toward the Parthenon, and at length standing before this monument of the one immortal Beauty, feeling his soul lifting towards this glorious form, realizing that he has gained that secret middle place from which radiate in vast circles all knowledge and all Beauty — and that he has arrived at the core and root of this beauty — who, lifting his eyes to the rhythmical succession of Doric columns, has felt "form" in its finest and noblest sense fulfill the spirit's highest want of form, that one will understand for what I am striving in my first dance tonight. It is my effort to express the feeling of the human body in relation to the Doric column.

For the last four months, each day I have stood before this miracle of perfection wrought of human hands. I have seen around it sloping the Hills, in many forms, but in direct contrast to them the Parthenon, expressing their fundamental idea. Not in imitation of the outside forms of nature, but in understanding of nature's great secret rules, rise the Doric columns.

The first days as I stood there my body was as nothing and my soul was scattered; but gradually called by the great inner voice of the Temple, came back the parts of my self to worship it: first came my soul and looked upon the Doric columns, and then came my body and looked — but in both were silence and stillness, and I did not dare to move, for I realized that of all the movements my body had made none was worthy to be made before a Doric Temple. And as I stood thus I realized that I must find a dance whose effort was to be worthy of this Temple — or never dance again.

Neither Satyr nor Nymph had entered here, neither Shadows nor Bacchantes. All that I had danced was forbidden this Temple — neither love nor hate nor fear, nor joy nor sorrow — only a rhythmic cadence, those Doric columns — only in perfect harmony this glorious Temple, calm through all the ages.

For many days no movement came to me. And then one day came the thought: These columns which seem so straight and still are not really straight, each one is curving gently from the base to the height, each one is in flowing movement, never resting, and the movement of each is in harmony with the others. And as I thought this my arms rose slowly toward the Temple and I leaned forward — and then I knew I had found my dance, and it was a Prayer.

ISADORA DUNCAN
The Art of the Dance, 1903–04

During the years directly preceding her accidental and untimely death in 1927, Isadora Duncan labored over My Life, *her autobiography. Reminiscing about her mystical experience at the Parthenon in 1903, she gives the reader a humorous self-portrait that is in every way remarkable.*

At Patras we had a hard struggle to decide between the attractions of Olympia and Athens, but a great, longing impatience for the Parthenon finally prevailed, and we took the train for Athens. The train sped through radiant Hellas. At one moment we glimpsed the snow-capped Olympus. At another we were surrounded by twisting, dancing nymphs and hamadryads of the olive groves. Our delight knew no bounds. Often our emotions were so violent that we could only find expression in tearful embraces. The stolid peasants at the little stations eyed us with wonder. They probably thought we were either drunk or crazy, whereas we were only exalted in our search for the highest and brightest of all wisdom — the blue eyes of Athena.

We arrived at violet-crowned Athens that evening, and the daybreak found us, with trembling limbs and hearts faint with adoration, ascending the steps of her Temple. As we mounted, it seemed to me that all the life I had known up to that time had fallen away from me as a motley garment; that I had never lived before; that I was born for the first time in that long breath and first gaze of pure beauty.

The sun was rising from behind Mount Pentelicus, revealing her marvellous clearness and the splendour of her marble sides sparkling in the sunlight. We mounted the last step of the Propylaea and gazed on the Temple shining in the morning light. With one accord we remained silent. We separated slightly from one another; for here was Beauty too sacred for words. It struck strange terror into our hearts. No cries or embraces now. We each found our vantage point of worship and remained for hours in an ecstasy of meditation which left us all weak and shaken.

We were now all together, my mother and her four children. We decided that the Clan Duncan was quite sufficient unto itself, that other people had only led us astray from our ideals. Also, upon viewing the Parthenon, it seemed to us that we had reached the pinnacle of perfection. We asked ourselves why we should ever leave Greece, since we found in Athens everything which satisfied our aesthetic sense . . . when I started on this pilgrimage, I had not had either the desire for fame nor for making money. It was purely a spiritual pilgrimage and it seemed to me that the spirit which I sought was the invisible Goddess Athena who still inhabited the ruined Parthenon. . . .

We had no desire to wander further. We had reached our Mecca, which, for us, meant the splendour of perfection — Hellas. I have since strayed from that first pure adoration of the wise Athena; and the last time I visited Athens, I confess that it was no longer her cult that attracted me, but rather the face of a suffering Christ in the little chapel of Daphnis. But at that time, in the morning of life, the Acropolis held for us all joy and inspiration. We were too strong, too defiant to understand pity.

Each dawn found us ascending the Propylon. We came to know the history of the sacred hill through all its successive periods. We brought our books and followed the history of each stone. We studied all the theories of distinguished archaeologists as to the origin and meaning of certain marks and portents. . . .

These events took place at the same time that I discovered our bank account was depleted. I remember the evening after the Royal performance I could not sleep and, at dawn, I went all by myself, to the Acropolis. I entered the Theatre of Dionysus and danced. I felt it was for the last time. Then I ascended the Propylaea and stood before the Parthenon. Suddenly it seemed to me as if all our dreams burst like a glorious bubble, and we were not, nor ever could be, other than moderns. We could not have the feeling of the Ancient Greeks. This Temple of Athena before which I stood, had in other times known other colours. I was, after all, but a Scotch-Irish-American. Perhaps through some affinity nearer allied to the Red Indian than to the Greeks.

ISADORA DUNCAN
My Life, 1927

REFERENCE

Chronology of Greek History

Entries in boldface refer to the Acropolis.

c. **5000** B.C. **Neolithic settlements on and around Acropolis**

c. 3000–1900   Migration of bronze-working peoples from east

c. 2200   Arrival of Greek-speaking people in Attica

c. 1600–1100   Athens becomes a center of Mycenaean culture; **palace built on Acropolis**

c. 1250–1200   Trojan War, with minor Athenian participation; signs of Mycenaean decline; **Acropolis fortified**

c. 1150–1100   End of Mycenaean civilization

c. 1100–800   Dark Age; arriving Dorians subjugate mainland Greece, only Athens holds out; Athenian *polis* develops as the typical Greek city

c. 750–650   Homer writes *Iliad* and *Odyssey;* beginnings of Archaic style in art; increasing class conflicts; emergence of hoplite phalanx

c. 650–510   Age of Tyrants

632   **Attempted coup by Cylon, who seizes Acropolis; his followers are starved into surrendering and then massacred**

620   Revision of the Athenian laws by Draco

c. 620–570   Growing political crisis

594   Solon made archon in Athens; he arbitrates between nobles and commoners, introduces reforms, encourages arts and crafts, and develops shipping

c. 570   First Athenian money coined

561–527   **Pisistratus seizes Acropolis;** as tyrant he initiates program for glorification of Athens under Athena; develops a civic ideal, invoking Pallas Athena, warrior-maiden and patroness of the arts, as city's special guardian; founds or embellishes city's most important festival, the Panathenaea; encourages cult of Dionysus

c. 550–500   Flowering of intellectual and artistic life in Ionia; rise of Persia; Ionian cities pass under Persian rule; some artists and intellectuals emigrate

527   Death of Pisistratus; his sons, Hippias and Hipparchus, assume power, make recitation of Homeric poems regular feature of Panathenaea

514   Harmodius, Aristogeiton assassinate Hipparchus

510   Hippias overthrown; **barricades himself on Acropolis;** surrenders and leaves Athens

508   Athenian constitution reformed by Cleisthenes

490   Persian invasion of Attica is repelled at Marathon by Athenians under Callimachus and Miltiades

489–480   **Construction of Older Parthenon is started;** at Themistocles's instigation, democratic reform of constitution and build-up of fleet carried out

480   Persian invasion; Spartan stand at Thermopylae; Persians sack Athens; **Older Parthenon destroyed; sacred olive tree of Athena burned;** Persians defeated by Athenian fleet off Salamis

479   Sack of Athens by Persians; Persians defeated at Plataea

479–449   Reconstruction of Athens; **temples on Acropolis deliberately left in ruins;** Athens organizes anti-Persian league

449   Peace with Persia; **Pericles initiates Acropolis temple-building program; Phidias commissioned to supervise overall project**

447–438   **A new Parthenon rises on the foundations of the Older Parthenon**

438   **Parthenon and Phidias's great statue of ivory and gold are dedicated to Athena**

437   **Construction of Propylaea begins**

431   **Propylaea virtually completed;** work suspended upon outbreak of war

431–404   Peloponnesian War pits Athens against Sparta; flowering of tragedy and comedy

430–429   Plague destroys a third of Athens's population

429   Pericles dies of plague

427–425   **Building of Callicrates's Temple of Athena Nike**

421   Peace of Nicias; **construction of Erechtheum**

415   Athenian expeditionary force under Alcibiades and Nicias invades Sicily, laying siege to Syracuse

413   Complete destruction of Athenian expeditionary force at Syracuse

411   Conservative revolution in Athens; **Aristophanes's *Lysistrata,* in which women seize Acropolis to force men to end war first produced**

410   Athenian fleet under Alcibiades wins victory at Cyzicus; **parapet of Athena Nike temple on Acropolis commissioned**

406   **Erechtheum completed**

404   Total defeat of Athens by Sparta; occupation by Spartans under Lysander; Long Walls leveled

403   Spartan withdrawal; restoration of democracy

399   Trial and execution of Socrates

394   Long Walls rebuilt

387   Peace treaty among Greek states dictated by Persia; Plato founds the Academy

Guide to Ancient Athens

The Athens of Pericles was surrounded by roughly circular defensive walls. The Athens of Roman times, built largely by Hadrian in the second century A.D., added a bulge to the eastern perimeter of the circle, but the city never grew to be much more than a mile wide in any direction. It is therefore possible to visit almost all of what remains of ancient Athens in a single day. A good place to start such a walking tour is at the **Dipylon Gate,** from which the Panathenaic processions set forth on their climb to the Acropolis. The most important landmarks of the ancient city can be seen along the **Panathenaic Way,** and what one misses en route is clearly visible from the Acropolis.

On the south side of the Panathenaic Way, around the Dipylon Gate, are ancient burial grounds known collectively as the **Ceramicus.** The older section lies within the city walls, but after the sixth century B.C. the dead were carried outside the walls and buried next to the road. The area was called the Ceramicus because of its proximity to the pottery makers' quarter, which extended all the way from the Dipylon Gate to the Agora, a distance of more than half a mile.

Houses along the way, as elsewhere in ancient Athens, were mostly one- and two-story structures with plain fronts. For Athenians, home life centered first and foremost on the interior courtyard. The furnishings of a typical house were few and simple, but choice, and even in the houses of the rich (at least until the fourth century) simplicity was the rule. Luxury and ostentation were frowned upon, and Pericles is said to have run his own household with great austerity.

Approaching the Agora from the northwest, along the Panathenaic Way, the visitor to ancient Athens next passed the metalworkers' quarter, its houses and workshops huddled on the slopes of the Agoraeus Colonus, or Agora Hill, which formed the west boundary of the Agora. On the broad crest of that hill stands the great **Temple of Hephaestus,** the god of metalworking and fire, which was begun just after the peace with Persia in 449 B.C. Dominating the Agora from above, it was until recent times called the Theseum because of its friezes representing the adventures of Theseus. Still impressive with its close ranks of Doric columns, the Hephaestus temple is the best preserved of all ancient Greek temples. Within its precincts stood bronze statues of Hephaestus and Athena Hephaestia, patron and patroness of metalworkers and armorers and of the commercial arts in general.

Continuing southeast, the Panathenaic Way enters the **Agora,** or marketplace. The Agora was the scene of nearly all Athenian business, large and small, and it was of equal importance as a social center. A square area roughly 150 yards across, the Agora was surrounded on all sides by rows of shops and civic offices set into the columned porches of long buildings called *stoas.* One of the largest of these, the **Stoa of Attalus,** which forms the east boundary of the Agora, faces the visitor entering the square from the northwest. The Stoa of Attalus has been completely restored and today houses a museum of archaeological finds from the Agora excavations that were begun in 1931.

At the north end of the Agora, visitors in ancient times could view the **Altar of the Twelve Gods.** From here official distances from Athens to other points in Attica were measured. A few steps eastward brought one to the famous **Painted Stoa,** with its murals (painted *c.* 460–450 B.C.) depicting Theseus's battle with the Amazons, the taking of Troy, and the victory over the Persians at Marathon in 490. After 300, the Painted Stoa gave its name to a new school of philosophy — Stoicism — for Zeno, its founder, taught here for more than fifty years. The Painted Stoa is thought to be at least partly intact, and excavations are currently being conducted by the American School of Classical Studies to locate it.

The other stoas surrounding the Agora were more or less identical to the Painted Stoa and the Stoa of Attalus with their long covered colonnades. There the men of Athens spent the days talking and doing business sheltered from sun and rain.

Across from the Stoa of Attalus was the **Stoa of Zeus,** also called the Royal Stoa, where the king archon, a magistrate concerned with religious affairs, presided. It was here that the charges leading to Socrates's death were instituted against him.

Next door to the Royal Stoa stood a small **Temple of Apollo,** and next to it stood the **Metroön,** which was dedicated to the mother of the gods and used as the city's record office, housing the Athenian state archives. Behind the Metroön was the **Bouleuterion,** the chamber in which the Council of the Five Hundred sat to draft laws for consideration by the Assembly. Many modern senate chambers have been modeled on the Bouleuterion's circular seating plan. Close by, at the southwest corner of the Agora, stood a circular building called

the **Tholos,** also used by members of the Council. Large stoas housing businesses and municipal offices likewise filled the south end of the Agora. In front of them stood the large **Odeon,** the music hall donated by Agrippa, son-in-law of Augustus Caesar.

Continuing past the music hall, the Panathenaic Way squeezes through the southeast corner of the Agora between two large stoas and a number of smaller business buildings and shrines. After a steady 300-yard climb up the northwest side of the Acropolis the Panathenaic Way enters the **Propylaea,** and continues across the top of the Acropolis past the **Erechtheum.** Beyond it lies the east entrance to the **Parthenon,** culminating point of the Panathenaic processions.

Periclean Athens did not extend far beyond the eastern end of the Acropolis. From this vantage point, one faces the Roman city built by Hadrian. The boundary, less than five hundred yards distant, is marked by **Hadrian's Arch,** which was erected by the Athenians to honor the great philhellene emperor. Consisting of two façades of superimposed arrangements in Corinthian style, the arch was completed by A.D. 131–32.

Nearby, roughly six hundred yards southeast of the Acropolis, stood the gigantic **Temple of Olympian Zeus.** This temple was begun by Pisistratus in the sixth century B.C. Resumed and half-completed in Hellenistic times, the temple excited admiration for hundreds of years before its actual dedication. Writing around the time of the birth of Christ, the Roman historian Livy said that it was the only Zeus temple in the world whose plan was proportionate to the majesty of the god. Some of its great

Corinthian columns were brought to Rome by Sulla following his sack of Athens in 86 B.C., and there they were incorporated into the magnificent Temple of Jupiter Capitolinus.

The honor of completing and dedicating the temple fell to Hadrian in A.D. 132. In a description of Athens written not long afterward, the traveler Pausanias noted that Hadrian placed inside the temple a statue of Olympian Zeus that surpassed all other statues in size save for the colossi at Rhodes and Rome. Made of ivory and gold, its workmanship was elegant considering the size, Pausanias observed. Next to the colossal Zeus stood a statue of Hadrian, and the temple grounds were filled with statues of Hadrian sent from every city of the Greek world. The Athenians' statue outdid them all, however, and Pausanias doubtless reflected the public opinion of his time when he wrote that despite the injury inflicted on the city by Sulla, Athens was flourishing thanks to Hadrian. Something of the temple's old grandeur may still be glimpsed in the surviving colonnade, which is tall and richly ornamented.

From the southeast wall of the Acropolis one can look straight down into the **Theater of Dionysus,** which witnessed the development of tragedy as a dramatic form. When it was built, barely a century had elapsed since the music of the Dionysian cult had evolved into the choral ode. From this in turn the first tragedies evolved, which were performed by one actor and a chorus. In the early days these plays were staged in the Agora, but throughout the fifth century they were given in the Theater of Dionysus, and it was there that the plays of

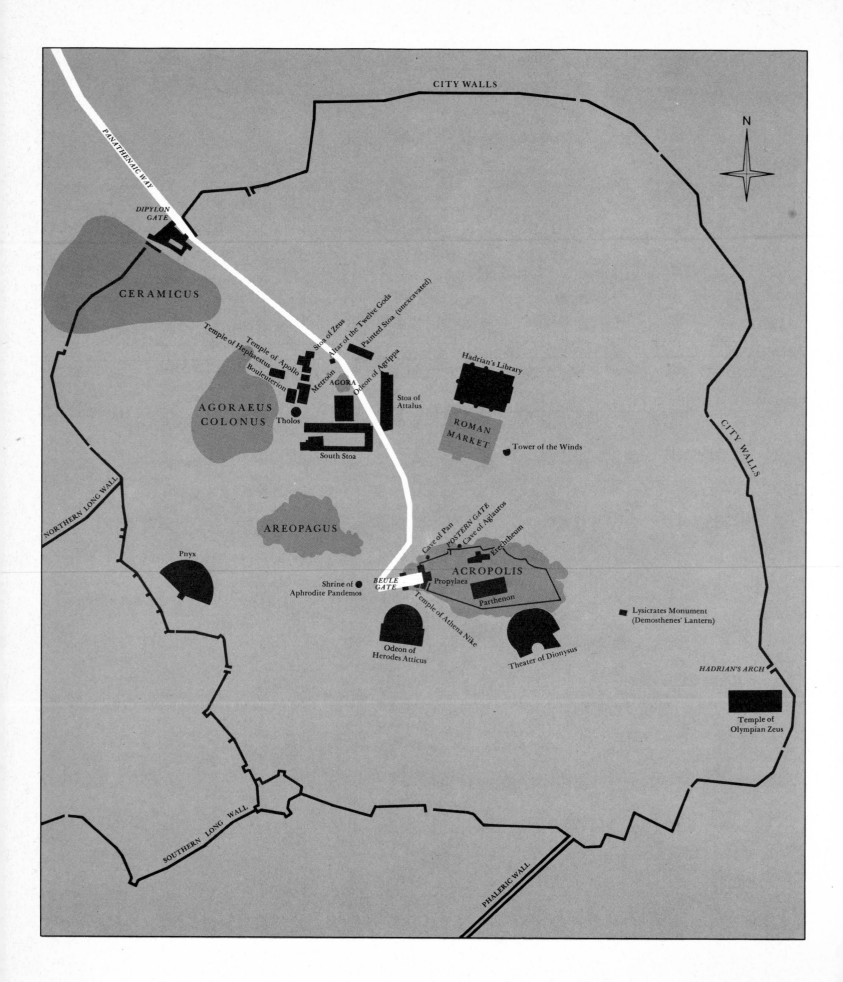

CITY WALLS

N

PANATHENAIC WAY

DIPYLON
GATE

CERAMICUS

Stoa of Zeus
Temple of Apollo
Altar of the Twelve Gods
Temple of Hephaestus
Painted Stoa (unexcavated)
Bouleuterion
Hadrian's Library
Metroön
Odeon of Agrippa
AGORA
Stoa of
Attalus
AGORAEUS
COLONUS
Tholos
ROMAN
MARKET
Tower of the Winds
South Stoa

CITY WALLS

NORTHERN LONG WALL

AREOPAGUS

Pnyx

Cave of Pan
POSTERN GATE
Cave of Aglauros
Erechtheum
ACROPOLIS
Shrine of
Aphrodite Pandemos
BEULE
GATE
Propylaea
Parthenon
Temple of Athena Nike

Lysicrates Monument
(Demosthenes' Lantern)

HADRIAN'S ARCH

Odeon of
Herodes Atticus

Theater of Dionysus

Temple of
Olympian Zeus

SOUTHERN LONG WALL

PHALERIC WALL

Aeschylus, Sophocles, Euripides, and Aristophanes were first presented.

Each year in March a predawn procession set out for this theater to open the city's festival of Dionysus. The spectacle was extraordinary: the wooden image of the god himself was carried by torchlight in a ship mounted on a wagon, accompanied by trumpeters and attendants bearing emblems of vegetation and fertility. The first of the day's three dramas, a tragedy, began at dawn; the afternoon was taken up with comedy. Seating capacity was more than 10,000, and in Periclean times the theater was always packed.

At the southwest foot of the Acropolis hill stands the **Odeon of Herodes Atticus.** Tutor of Marcus Aurelius, curator of the Panathenaic festival, and noted philanthropist, Herodes Atticus was the generous benefactor of many sites in Greece, but he loved Athens best of all, and he left many tangible proofs of his love. The best preserved of these is the Odeon, now used for performances of the annual Athens Festival.

Looking west from the Acropolis, a visitor to ancient Athens could see the Long Walls (the north and middle walls extending to Piraeus, and the south wall to Phaleron) which served to protect Athens's lifeline to the sea.

Just inside the city's walls and some five hundred yards due west of the Propylaea lay the hill of the **Pnyx.** The meeting place of the Athenian Assembly, of which all adult male citizens were members, the Pnyx was the scene of all the great debates on matters of law and policy. It was here that Pericles won adoption of his great Acropolis building program. (Each October the Pnyx

was closed to men for three days and consecrated to the Thesmophoria, a fertility festival for women only, honoring the earth mother Demeter and her daughter Persephone.)

Northeast of the Pnyx rises the **Areopagus,** or Hill of Ares, the seat of the aristocratic governing body in early Athens. The Areopagus Council, which combined administrative, judicial, and religious functions, dated from Homeric times. According to Aeschylus, the Council was created by Athena in order to judge Orestes for the murder of his mother. With the rise of democracy, its powers were greatly reduced, and by Pericles's generation its jurisdiction was limited to cases of premeditated murder, poisoning, arson, certain religious questions, and the care of the sacred olive trees. It was before the Council of the Areopagus that St. Paul was brought in A.D. 54 to explain his doctrine — after he had spent some time explaining it in the streets of Athens. To the Council he delivered the Homily on the Unknown God — and was politely dismissed.

If one proceeds to the north side of the Acropolis, one can see the **Roman Market** and just beyond it **Hadrian's Library.** The former consists of a large courtyard surrounded by columned porticoes. Built around the time of Christ with money donated by Julius Caesar and Augustus, it became the eastern end of a new marketplace that grew up after A.D. 267, when the Agora was destroyed along with much of the city of Athens by a migrating Germanic people, the Herulian Goths. At the east side of the Roman Market stands an octagonal tower of white marble covered with sculptured friezes. Commonly known

as the **Tower of the Winds,** it rises to a height of almost forty feet. Built in Hellenistic times, it was originally a hydraulic clock equipped with sundials and a weathercock. Its interior mechanism was lost long ago, and with it the memory of the clock.

Just north of the Roman Market lie the ruins of Hadrian's Library, designed to harmonize with the plan and dimensions of the market. It had several porticoed galleries in Corinthian style and sumptuously ornate reading and lecture rooms.

Looking north from the Acropolis, one sees mountains everywhere — the long ridge of Mount Parnes forming the natural frontier that separates Attica from Boeotia, and of course Mount Pentelicus. Under the brightness and purity of the Aegean sky, Pentelicus's slopes still gleam with scars inflicted 2,500 years ago when the marble for the Parthenon was quarried there.

Selected Bibliography

Bowra, Cecil M. *The Greek Experience*. Cleveland: World Publishing Co., 1957.

Burn, A. R. *Persia and the Greeks*. London: E. Arnold Ltd., 1962.

Cary, Max. *A History of the Greek World, 323 to 146 B.C.* 2nd. rev. ed. London: Methuen & Co., Ltd., 1963.

Dinsmoor, William Bell. *The Architecture of Ancient Greece*. London: B. T. Batsford Ltd., 1950.

Flaceliere, R. *Daily Life in Greece at the Time of Pericles*. Translated by Peter Green. London: Weidenfeld & Nicolson Ltd., 1965.

Green, Peter. *The Year of Salamis, 480–479 B.C.* New York: Praeger Publishers, 1970.

Hill, Ida C. *The Ancient City of Athens*. London: Methuen & Co., Ltd., 1953.

Hopper, R. J. *The Acropolis*. New York: The Macmillan Co., 1971.

Lang, M. and Eliot, C. W. J. *The Athenian Agora: A Guide to the Excavation and Museum*. 2nd ed. Princeton: Princeton University Press, 1962.

MacKendrick, Paul. *The Greek Stones Speak*. New York: St. Martin's Press, 1962.

Paton, J. M., ed. *The Erechtheum*. Cambridge, Mass.: Harvard University Press, 1927.

St. Clair, W. *Lord Elgin and the Marbles*. Oxford: Oxford University Press, 1967.

Woodhouse, C. M. *The Story of Modern Greece*. London: Faber and Faber Ltd., 1968.

Acknowledgments and Picture Credits

The Editors make grateful acknowledgment for the use of excerpted material from the following works:

Journal of a Visit to Europe and the Levant, October 11, 1856–May 6, 1857 by Herman Melville. Edited by Howard C. Horsford. Copyright © 1955 by Princeton University Press. The excerpt appearing on page 150 is reproduced by permission of Princeton University Press.

My Life by Isadora Duncan. Copyright renewed 1955 by Liveright Publishing, New York. The excerpt appearing on pages 159–60 is reproduced by permission of Liveright Publishing.

The Art of Dance by Isadora Duncan. Copyright © 1928 by Helen Hackett, Inc., Copyright © 1969 by Theatre Arts Books. The excerpt appearing on page 159 is reprinted by permission of Theatre Arts Books, New York.

The Editors would like to express their particular appreciation to David G. Rattray for compiling The Parthenon in Literature, *the guide to ancient Athens, and the chronology of Greek history and to John Veltri for his creative photography. In addition, the Editors would like to thank the following organizations and individuals:*

Acropolis Museum, Athens — George Dontas, Director

American School of Classical Studies, Athens — Spiro Spiropolous, Eugine Vanderpool, Jr.

Department of Antiquities and Restoration, Athens — Spiros Marinatos

National Archaeological Museum, Athens

Norman A. Doenges — Dartmouth College

Barbara Nagelsmith, Paris

Lynn Seiffer, New York

Jehane West, Athens

Monica Wilson, Rome

The title or description of each picture appears after the page number (boldface), followed by its location. Photographic credits appear in parentheses. The following abbreviations are used:

(JV) — John Veltri
AM — Acropolis Museum
ASCS — American School of Classical Studies
BM — Benaki Museum, Athens
MMA — Metropolitan Museum of Art, New York
NAM — National Archaeological Museum

ENDPAPERS Inner colonnade of the Parthenon. (John Veltri) HALF TITLE Symbol designed by Jay J. Smith Studio FRONTISPIECE The Acropolis. (John Veltri) **9** Gold wreath, 4th century B.C. BM (JV) **10–11** Frieze figures of Heracles, Demeter, and Persephone, from the Elgin Marbles. British Museum (Russell Ash) **12–13** Bronze statue of Athena, mid-4th century B.C. NAM (JV)

CHAPTER I **14** Marble figurine of a Cycladic mother-goddess, *c.* 2400 B.C. NAM (JV) **16** Stone foundations of the Acropolis. (John Veltri) **17** Attic coin, *c.* 450–440 B.C. American Numismatic Society **18** Fragment from an archaic building on the Acropolis. AM (JV) **19** Ivory jewel box,

CHAPTER VII **118** Stele inscribed with law against tyranny, 336 B.C. ASCS (JV) **120** Inscribed regulations from the Library of Pantainos. ASCS **121** Odeon of Herodes Atticus. (John Veltri) **122** Icon of St. George, by Emmanuel Tzanes, 1659. Byzantine Museum, Athens (JV) **123** Jewelry from the Byzantine period. BM (JV) **124** Byzantine ivory of St. Constantine, 10th century. Dumbarton Oaks Collection, Washington, D.C. **124–25** Early Christian capital, from the Church of St. George. ASCS **125** Detail of Justinian, from the Barberini Ivory, *c.* 527. Louvre **126** Temple of Hephaestus. (John Veltri) **128–29** Drawing of the Acropolis, by Verneda, 1670. British Museum; right, Engraving of the 1687 explosion in the Parthenon, from F. Fanelli's *Athene Attica*, 1707. British Museum **130–31** Painting of the Acropolis at the beginning of the 19th century, by Thomas Horner. BM **133** Greek villagers in Metsovo, 1969. (John Veltri) **135** Aerial view of Athens with Acropolis in foreground. (Charles E. Rotkin)

THE PARTHENON IN LITERATURE **136** The Apotheosis of Homer, 2nd-3rd century B.C. British Museum **138–60** Twelve drawings of the Parthenon friezes, from a series once attributed to Jacques Carrey. All: Bibliothèque Nationale, Paris.

REFERENCE **165** Map by Francis & Shaw, Inc.

Index